ONE CHURCH
ONE FAITH
ONE LORD

RENÉ GIRAULT

ONE CHURCH
ONE FAITH
ONE LORD

New perspectives in ecumenism

ST PAULS

ST PAULS
Middlegreen, Slough SL3 6BT, United Kingdom
Moyglare Road, Maynooth, Co. Kildare, Ireland

English translation © ST PAULS 1993

ISBN 085439 425 7

Printed in the EEC by Loader Jackson Printers, Arlesey

ST PAULS is an activity of the priests and brothers of the Society of St Paul
who proclaim the Gospel through the media of social communication

CONTENTS

Abbreviations used in notes throughout

DC   *Documentation Catholique*
BIP   *Bulletin d'Information Protestant*
SOP *Service Orthodoxe de Presse*
BSS *Bulletin d'Information* in association with BIP,
            SOP and SNOP (Service National d'Opinion
            Publique)
UDC *Unité des Chrétiens*
BEM *Baptéme, Eucharistie et Ministère*

Preface

IN these times when ecumenism does not always seem to be breaking new ground, I would like to ask my fellow Christians if they are paying enough attention to what is happening in their Churches at the present moment. Some, to be sure, are complacent in their sectarian triumphalism, and don't really want to listen. They hardly lose any sleep over the scandal of the divided Churches. Fortunately, there are others who are full of good will and who want to build the *one Church* again. But they often come up against a difficulty: they feel that their Church has now gone to the limit of its possibilities and that taking any further step would be betraying it. It is especially with these people in mind that this book has been written: to show them that new ways are being explored.

There are *four ways in which the realization of unity can be understood.* Here we will consider what is new and this will shed light on all the rest.

The following chapters will be an invitation to a *widening of outlook both in time and in space.* To understand what is happening, we need to know the history of the separations and the reunions, with their ebb and flow, and the great ground swell of ecumenism, which is now irreversible. We need also to reach beyond the closed horizon of our accustomed parishes, and to take an interest in *all the Churches.* With a new Europe in the making, Catholics are entering into greater dialogue with the members of the Reformed Churches, while the Anglicans in Britain are establishing closer contacts with the members of the Orthodox Church in Romania and Russia. All the Churches, with their intricate mosaic of heritages are now bonded one to another, listening together to what the Spirit is saying to them in our times.

I would like to specify that, as a Catholic, the 'place' from which I observe and speak can only be the Church to which I belong and whose priest I am. The various ecumenical ministries I have exercised have, however, continually widened my fraternal outlook towards the life of the different Churches, which I have understood better and often admired without losing my own identity. For seeking authentically the Lord's will and his ways is something to be done both in love and in truth.

I would also like to emphasize that the convictions expressed here are in no way my personal ideas; they are simply a record of the search that is taking place – somewhat confusedly at times – in the living Churches of today. My work has only been to tie together the intertwining threads of intuitions, initiatives and striking convergences into a coherent whole. Of course, all synthesis is risky, for even the immediate future always holds surprises in store. But now, we can already glimpse the shape of ecumenism to come.

Chapter 1

Four ways of envisaging the achievement of Christian unity

AS Christians of the twentieth century, we were born into separated Churches and we know that this division among Christians is a scandal to the world. We also know that our age is one of great longing for unity and that a slow reconstruction of this unity is in process. It is the aim of this present work to take stock of its progress. We begin with those points that will help to put in proper perspective the existing separation and its seriousness.

First, a distinction has to be made between the *confrontations* that exist within a Church and the actual *split* between the Churches. Christians may be tempted to make light of the present divisions among the major Churches, by thinking that they have always existed and that the New Testament itself gives witness of such a situation. We must be very clear on this point. It is quite true that the first Christian communities were troubled by internal conflict. If the first Christian community had "but one heart and one soul" (Acts 4:32), we know that this idyllic description has never completely corresponded to the reality. For in the same book of the Acts of the Apostles and the Letters of St Paul, we find the echo of dramatic tensions which sometimes disturbed the communities. However, these crises were not such ruptures of unity as to bring about the separation of the Churches.

Alongside these internal tensions, there were, however, serious differences right from the beginning. This was the position in the first century of the Christians known as 'Judaizers' who were condemned at the Council of Jerusalem in the year 50 AD. They claimed that pagans converted

9

to Christianity should, before receiving baptism, proceed by the traditional path of circumcision and the observance of the Jewish law. Yet again, in the second century the Marcionites, whose leader Marcion was excommunicated in the year 144, went to the opposite extreme – they wished to repress in Christianity every reference to the Old Testament. In these and other cases, in which the dissension touched the core of the faith, or when a decree of condemnation appeared necessary and was not accepted by all, divisions did occur and separated Churches were formed alongside the main Church. These early divisions, however, are no longer a cause of concern for us today, for these separated Churches, after a moment of prosperity, eventually withered away and disappeared. The memory of them simply reminds us to be vigilant, for the temptations which engendered them are continually coming to life again.

Yet, there still exist three major divisions which have survived to our own day:

1. those of the fifth century, with the establishing of the Eastern Churches;

2. those of the eleventh century with the break between the West and the Eastern Orthodox Church;

3. those of the sixteenth century, following in the wake of the Reformation in the West, with the rise of the Protestant Churches.

From the outset we must insist on the seriousness of these divisions which are obviously a contradiction to the proclamation of the Gospel. Let us think of all those people of good will who, from the outside, look at our separated Churches, and quietly compare them to the great world religions. They can only conclude, with a shaking of the head, that from the point of view of the Church as a sign of unity, we hardly present a good image.

We must take it even further. Before any comparison with other groups of believers, the division of the Churches is in itself a kind of treason, for it is a negation by the Christian community of its deepest meaning which is to be a living reflection of the Trinity. This point is forcibly recalled by a theologian who is also an apostle of unity, "The unity of believers does not arise solely from the harmony of *fraternal charity*... Neither does it belong uniquely to *missionary logic*... It is immediately related to the *glory of God*."[1] If we do not agree to this at the beginning, the difficult analyses which follow may be like the subtle analytical games of theologians. We must, therefore, begin by fully accepting the fundamental word of Christ who gives us both the challenge, the definition and the method, "Father, may they be one in us, as you are in me and I am in you, so that the world may believe it was you who sent me" (Jn 17:21).

The separation of the Churches is no ordinary event arising out of the vicissitudes of history, it is a betrayal of the gospel, involving a degree of sinfulness. The re-establishment of unity will not be of the order of negotiation or diplomacy, nor the conclusion of analyses of situations and debates about ideas. It will demand, primarily, conversion and repentance. The contemplation of the Trinity and meditation on the prayer of Christ for unity are the first sources of any Christian approach to a search for unity.

It is at this deep level of conscience that the disunity of Christians has tormented people of faith of every century. Let us listen to the plaintive cry of Cardinal Bessarion at the time when the Council of Florence in the fifteenth century was trying to re-establish unity between East and West:

What excuse can we offer to justify our unwillingness to unite? What answer have we to give to God to justify our divisions with our brethren, when to unite us and to bring us back to the one fold, he himself came down from heaven, became incarnate and was crucified? What excuse can we make to our descendants? Even more so to our contemporaries?[2]

Bessarion preached in a desert. More than half a millennium has passed, but East and West are still separated and the West is itself divided.

> To the faults against unity the testimony of St John can also be applied: "If we say we have not sinned, we make God a liar, and his word is not in us" (1 Jn 1:10). Thus in humble prayer we beg pardon of God and of our separated brethren, just as we forgive those who offend us.
>
> Vatican Council II, *Decree on ecumenism*, no. 7

The Churches have never resigned themselves to these divisions and two of the major signs of our time are the consciousness of the urgency for the unity of the Churches and the serious effort towards it. Who could be insensitive to the appeal which was launched as long as 30 years ago by the preacher at the great September Assembly in the Cevennes? He had begun by recalling, as was done each year, what had been the first vocation of the Reformation. Then, breaking the usual customs, he added forcefully, "Has not God the permission to ask us, four centuries on, another question?... I remain convinced that the question that God is asking the Church of our time is indeed the question of unity."[3]

Who could be unimpressed by what Pope John Paul II said in his address to his collaborators, cardinals and members of the Roman Curia, on the twentieth anniversary of the conclusion of the Second Vatican Council?

> This movement comes from the Holy Spirit and I feel deeply responsible to him. I humbly ask for his light and his strength so as better to serve this holy cause of unity. I ask you to implore this grace with me, to implore it for me. I would repeat that it is with an irrevocable decision that the Catholic Church became involved in the ecumenical movement and that she wishes to contribute to it in every way she can. As Bishop of Rome, I consider it one of my pastoral priorities.[4]

One could multiply quotations of this kind.

Now, it is possible to be in agreement on the urgency of the situation while still being divided about the means and method of solving the problem. By slightly exaggerating the characteristics, we can distinguish four ways of envisaging unity between the Churches. These four different ways have appeared successively and are still collectively present today. We shall look at them in turn, with their characteristics, their arguments and their limitations. They are:

1. *Unity by 'absorption' of other Churches*. This view was for a long time the one ruling idea. It is now outmoded but has not completely disappeared.

2. *The unity willed by Christ, in the time and by the means that he wishes*. This view coincided with the appearance of ecumenism which was like the opening of a doorway. It is the most widespread view at present and needs to continue.

3. *'Unity in plurality', by accepting one another as we are*. A recent attractive viewpoint which, however, is still static and could be a subtle and unconscious form of absorption.

4. *An evangelical conversion of all the Churches through listening to each other's questions*. A point of view still badly formulated, but there are many signs which tend to favour it as the way for the future.

1. Unity by 'absorption' of other Churches

This concept of 'absorption' was for a long time universally regarded as the only possible solution since each Church had the conviction that it, and it alone, had the whole truth. How could a Church have honestly imagined that unity was possible outside the acceptance of this unique truth? The reasoning of each of the great Churches, with some simplification, was very similar.

The Catholic Church, as it watched the currents of the

Reformation, had an argument as simple as it was irrefutable. In the sixteenth century, it reasoned, the Protestants left and divided the West. Enclosed in their errors and deprived of the charism of the truth, they divided themselves into a multitude of rival denominations. They must, therefore, renounce their errors and return, all of them, to the great Church which has awaited them for centuries. This was the language of the Encyclical *Mortalium Animos* of Pius XI in 1928, "The union of Christians cannot be otherwise realized than by favouring the return of the dissidents to the one and true Church of Christ, which they had formerly the misfortune to abandon. Let them therefore return to the common Father. He will welcome them with all his tenderness."[5]

On their side, the Churches of the Reformation reasoned, with the same logic, in exactly the opposite way. The Catholic Church, they thought, refused to reform itself in the sixteenth century. It continues to remain outside evangelical purity and has further enlarged the gap with new dogmas! Let it finally reform itself, and thus unity will be achieved with us! In 1948, Karl Barth proclaimed, "Our only attitude with regard to Catholicism is one of mission, of evangelization!"[6]

Likewise, in its far eastern reaches, the Orthodox Church, when it looked westward, could not avoid thinking: If there is one thing that no one can deny, it is that our Church has remained entirely faithful to its origins. The best proof is that we are even accused of being too immobile! It is in the West that the various Churches have deviated from the authentic faith of their origins: the Catholics have added to revelation, the Protestants have whittled it down. Let them rediscover then, all of them, the faith of their origins, and there will be unity with us! Again in 1982, the holy monks of Mount Athos reminded the new Orthodox Metropolitan of Switzerland that its mission was to bring "the witness of the Orthodox faith among the Christians of the other confessions separated from the Church of Christ, so that they become aware of their errors and return to Orthodoxy."[7]

However, we must be aware of a condescending attitude towards the various Churches' reactions. For each Church considers that it is faithful to the Gospel. The underlying metaphor is that of the lost child of the parable whose return we await and who will be welcomed with love.

Nevertheless, we must recognize that this secular attitude has not brought about unity. Bloody confrontation or peaceful co-existence, violent polemic or irenic controversy have traversed history without appreciable result. Each Church has ended by recognizing that it is not alone in believing that it is possessor of the whole truth. The troubling fact is, that the others, standing firmly on their positions and lost in their own beliefs, have apparently produced good fruit. Was it not the place to apply the reasoning of Gamaliel (Acts 5:38-39)? If the other Churches were but human enterprises, they would have disappeared of their own accord. If they have survived, is it not because they have some mysterious connection with God's design?

Thinking in this way, a new perception of the truth begins to emerge. Is it possible to describe it as something that we 'possess'? Is not the truth rather a mystery into which we enter and of which we never cease discovering the depth? For, if Christ is the Truth, is it not rather this Truth which possesses us?

Hence, one day, ecumenism was born, a new word (at least as a substantive, since we already used the adjective 'ecumenical') which, Yves Congar tells us, appeared about 1920-21, adding that when a new word appears, it is a new reality that has been born.[8] With this reality appeared a new conception of the search for Christian unity.

2. The unity willed by Christ

Probably the best way to express this new concept of unity is to go back to the novel formula invented by Abbé Couturier, a priest of Lyons, in 1935-1937. In 1908, two Anglicans Spencer Jones and Lewis Thomas Wattson, who later became Catholic, suggested having an octave of prayer, between the feast of the Chair of Peter at Rome and the Conversion of St Paul (18-25 January), to ask God for the return of dissidents to the true Church, which for them was the Catholic Church. This prayer, which arose from a vision of 'absorption', was immediately accepted by the Catholic Church and by certain Anglo-Catholic circles, but did not spread to other Churches. The same was true of the world week of prayer for unity launched by the Evangelical Alliance, which still holds it in the first week in January, and which was anti-Catholic.

Keeping to the idea of a week of prayer with the same dates of 18 to 25 January, Abbé Couturier proposed a new formula which was radically different. We should, he said, pray for "the unity which Christ wills, in the time and by the means he chooses". Each Church could associate itself with this petition while preserving its convictions and admitting that none of us knows the entire will of the Lord in this matter.

In spite of the inevitable resistance met by most new ideas, the prayer formula spread gradually to all the Catholic dioceses. It was a formula which corresponded to the intuitions of the other Churches, especially the Reformed, in which ecumenism was already at work. At last, there was a move away from the idea of absorption and 'unionism'.

This dawning ecumenism led to two realizations. The first was the delighted discovery of the other Churches and of all that we could do together with them. Churches which had fought, or at best ignored, each other, now began to meet, pray and read the Bible together. By working together they began to see each other with new eyes. Even though this involved only a few people at first, the phenomenon was striking and soon spread. At times, people began to dream of a unity just round the corner. With the accelerated pace of history, why should this generation of pioneers not be the one to see unity restored?

However, this optimistic vision soon gave place to a

second, more sobering realization. If Christian unity lies in the order of mystery, it is not only because we do not know when or how it will come about, but also because, the Churches being what they are, there are still profound contradictions, which seem more and more insurmountable, the further we advance. In a Lenten sermon in 1946, Pastor Marc Boegner made a telling comment which was to meet with widespread agreement, "Let us not delude ourselves, the Churches of the Reformation and the Catholic Church have such totally opposed views on certain essential issues that they could not renounce them without betraying what is, in the eyes of each, the truth of the Gospel. It is their right, indeed their duty to hold to these views without compromise."[9]

Lest we should lose hope at this point, let us always remember that "the walls of disunity do not reach up to heaven". Quoting those words of an Orthodox bishop, Plato of Kiev, Boegner added those of a Catholic, Père de Foucauld, who reminded us that Jesus is the "master of the impossible", and concluded with the Gospel that "what is impossible to human beings is possible to God" (Luke 18:27). It is Jesus who will give us the gift of unity when we are ready for it. It is for us to prepare ourselves by coming together and doing together that our conscience allows us to do together – which can be a great deal.

Even if there were still insurmountable barriers between the Churches, a great step forward had been taken. There was new hope, and it now seemed possible to undertake immense tasks together, starting straight away. A whole ecumenical generation lived by this vision, devoting themselves untiringly to it, conscious that in this way they were laying the foundations of a unity which would come in its time as the gift of God.

However, was it not possible to do more? Ever more closely united by prayer, study and joint activity, the ecumenists felt that the time was ripe to take a further step forward by tackling the problem from a different angle.

3. Unity in plurality

This new way of envisaging unity has recently emerged in certain Reformed Churches and among Catholics close to them, especially the partners in mixed marriages. Their reasoning was as follows: these supposedly insurmountable barriers which have separated us for centuries, are they still real? We now feel so close to one another that sometimes we wonder why we are still separated. Let us take a good look at one another: we respect each other, we are discovering each other afresh, sometimes we even admire each other, and we have begun to love one another again! We can do nearly everything together and we feel comfortable when we attend a eucharistic celebration in the other Church. So why not take one last step by sharing the Eucharist freely and telling ourselves that those famous 'insurmountable' barriers are no longer there. We are a Church which is invisibly united, but plural in its outward and visible form!

This is essentially the solution proposed by Oscar Cullmann in a book with the significant title *Unity through diversity*, "What I suggest is a community of completely autonomous Churches which would remain Catholic, Protestant, Orthodox, keeping the gifts the Spirit has given them, not in order to turn in on themselves, but to form a communion of all those who call on the name of Jesus Christ."[10]

There is a real and laudable progress represented by this viewpoint which has a much broader vision than the notion of absorption into uniformity. Moreover, this attitude is firmly based on the New Testament in which we can already see a plurality of ideas and ecclesiastical organizations, some of whose features even appear contradictory![11] Yet as it stands, this new attitude is neither acceptable to the Catholic Church, nor to the Orthodox Church, nor to many Protestants.

Let us take a closer look at it. By this sort of reasoning, is one not, in fact, dismissing the problem in an artificial

18

way? As long as the differences are considered to be divisive, even by one of the partners – as is the case in the very way we conceive of the Church – can we honestly behave as if these differences did not exist and go ahead to announce some kind of cheap unity? In the last analysis, isn't this a rather lazy solution to the problem, to take each other just as we are, remaining quietly self-satisfied and mutually tolerant? ("I don't ask you to change, don't ask me to change either and let's live in peace!") There might even be a suspicion here of an unconscious return to the idea of surreptitious 'absorption', with a somewhat Protestant bias, as the Protestant concept of the Church would lend itself most easily to the idea of plural unity.

Yet, now we seem to be going round in circles. Which way forward is left to us, which is not the old absorption, nor the present status quo transformed into plural unity, nor the endless waiting at the foot of those insurmountable barriers? It is precisely this way forward that is being sought in this last way of envisaging the achievement of unity.

4. Evangelical conversion of Churches

This new way, now being discovered, is that which asks us all to examine our consciences by listening to the profound questions of others, so we may be more faithful to the Gospel and so come to full communion through diversity. What does this involve?

In one sense, we could keep to the intuition behind the third way of looking at unity, as long as we expand it further. We could say something like, "Let us take each other as we are, along with the serious questions we ask each other in the name of the Gospel." We would soon see that, having taken those questions into account, we would be in a very different position from where we are today.

It may well be asked, why didn't we think of this before? Perhaps we would have to reply that the slowness of present-day Christians in thinking of it, is in itself instructive. It is only by gradual degrees that people realize that to address the accusations of others does not mean denying one's own truth; it also takes time to see that mutual questioning does not necessarily mean total opposition. For, we are beginning to realize that the serious questions involved are less opposed than crossed, so each Church can, and indeed ought, to listen to the challenge of the other, without thereby denying its own truth and realizing that it is a love of that truth which impels it to ask its own questions.

It is a matter, for all concerned, of a deeper conversion to the Gospel; no one could possibly find fault with that. The novelty is that this conversion is prompted by the questioning of the other Churches, in an atmosphere of mutual attention and respect. It is a conversion not primarily of individuals, but of whole Churches. This is why many people refer to this ecclesiastical 'conversion' by the Greek term *metanoia*, to avoid any confusion with the notion of an individual's conversion.[12]

Naturally, any novelty often meets with some initial suspicion, and at first the Churches wondered anxiously if they might not be led unwittingly to sacrifice the very things which were essential to their identity, and so to their faithfulness. This prudent reaction was healthy. However, experience shows that the farther off one is, the more wary one feels! In fact, people began to see that the whole process had already started, and that the Catholic Church was not the last to join in.

We could say that Vatican II provided a starting-point, with its invitation to 'observers' from the other Churches, who were not only asked to 'observe' the debates but to relay their comments, which were of great help in composing the conciliar schemas. Basically, the Council justified such a procedure by reminding us that "Christ summons the Church, as she goes her pilgrim way, to that continual reformation of which she always has need, insofar as she is a human institution here on earth". It went on to specify the areas to which this applies: "conduct, Church discipline, or even the formulation of doctrine

20

(which must be carefully distinguished from the deposit of faith itself)".[13]

We have a link here with one of the insights of the Reformation, which gave it its name, "The Church reformed, and always in need of reform" (*Ecclesia reformata, semper reformanda*). Pastor Hébert Roux, official observer for the Reformed World Alliance, was always clear on this point. In his turn, he appealed to his own Church, even before the decree had been put to the vote, "If we wish to be faithful (to the spirit of the Reformation), when we see the Catholic Church examining itself and allowing others to question it, we should do likewise."[14]

In the same vein, a recent document published by the Evangelical World Alliance, while vigorously criticizing the Catholic Church, declares that the Spirit is nevertheless at work in the life of its faithful, and concludes, "The best way to act in the face of Catholicism in its present state of ferment, is to lend an attentive ear to the Word of God and the Spirit of God in order to effect our own reform."[15]

Even the Orthodox Church is not at rest. Preaching in Geneva in 1986, the Patriarch of Antioch, Ignatius IV, declared, "The dictum *ecclesia semper reformanda* has a strangely contemporary ring for the Orthodox Church!"[16] An Orthodox theologian wrote recently that the Holy Spirit is rousing us "to combat the deadness of our institutions, rites and language insofar as that language is repetitive, that tradition mere traditionalism, leading us to cut ourselves off from the needs of men and women today."[17]

The ecumenical scene abounds in examples of these new attitudes. In order to find them, we just have to keep our ears open. Throughout the following pages, we shall see the effect of these attitudes, notably in the great dialogues now taking place between all the Churches.

NOTES

1. Jean M.R. Tillard, "L'oecuménisme, une exigence spirituelle", *UDC*, July 1980, p. 26.
2. Mansi, *Sacrorum conciliorum nova et amplissima collectio*, vol. 31 A, col. 963, Venice 1798 and Paris-Leipzig 1906.
3. Sermon by Pastor Jean Valette, 3 September 1961. In *Foi et vie*, nos. 5-6, 1961, p. 41.
4. Address to the cardinals of the Roman Curia, 28 June 1985, *DC*, 4 August 1985.
5. *DC*, 28 January 1928, col. 202. This doctrine of the 'return' persisted in the Catholic Church until Vatican II. After that, there were various changes of attitude on this subject, even though the word 'return' recurs in a context which shows a completely opposite stance (as in the meeting of Paul VI with Athenagoras, at Jerusalem in 1964. Cf *DC*, 2 February 1964, col. 179). The conciliar decree speaks of the 'recomposition' of Christian unity.
6. Quoted by Pastor Hébert Roux in *De la désunion vers la communion*, Centurion 1981, p. 199.
7. *Episkepsis*, 1 December 1982, p. 8. The same attitude may be found among the representatives of the neo-Greek Orthodox movement. Cf the pages on the 'Western deviation' of the presentation of the Christian faith by the Greek theologian, Christos Yannaras, *La foi vivante de l,Église: introduction à la théologie orthodoxe*, Athens 1983 and Paris, Cerf 1989, p. 177ff.
8. Yves Congar, "Chrétiens en dialogue", collection *Unam sanctam*, no. 50, Cerf 1964, p. 90.
9. Marc Boegner, *Le probléme de l'unité chrétienne*, Je Sers editions, 1946, pp. 103-105.
10. Oscar Cullmann, *L'unité par la diversité*, Cerf, 1986, p. 47.
11. Max-Alain Chevallier, "L'unité plurielle de l'Église d'aprés le Nouveau Testament" in *Revue d'histoire et de philosophie religieuse*, January-March 1986, p. 47.
12. The word *metanoia* applied, not to individual conversion, but to the transformation of the community, appears in 1974 in Rome, in a conference held at the Institute of St Anselm, sponsored by the Pontifical University and the Institute for Ecumenical Research in Strasbourg (a part of the Lutheran World Federation). Cf "Unitatis redintegratio", 1964-1974. The impact of the "Decree on ecumenism", edited by G. Bèkés and V. Vajda, *Studia Anselmiana*, no. 71, p. 161.
13. *Decree on ecumenism*, no. 6.
14. Hébert Roux, *Le concile et le dialogue oecuménique*, Seuil 1964, p. 165. Cf Karl Barth's remarks in *The ecumenical review*, July 1963. Cf *DC* 15 September 1963, col. 1226-1227.
15. *Regards sur le catholicisme contemporain*, booklet published by the French Evangelical Alliance, 1990, p. 21.
16. *Episkepsis*, 15 January 1987.
17. Boris Bobrinskoy, *Tradition sacrée et traditions humaines* (Conference at the Institute of Saint Sergius), in *SOP*, April 1990, p. 27.

Chapter 2

How the Churches awoke to ecumenism

THE unsuccessful and short-lived attempts made by the Councils of Lyons (1274) and Florence (1439) to achieve a temporary unity between East and West had left a bitter taste, and the two halves of Christianity continued to live mindful of the anathemas hurled at each other. In the West, where the violent clashes of the Wars of Religion and their manifold consequences had gradually given place to more peaceful controversies, the opposing theologies, hardened by polemics, confronted each other. Church organization reflected division – fragmentation in the Reformed Churches contrasted with ever growing centralization in the Catholic Church.

However, from the middle of the nineteenth century, one can perceive the beginning of a change in thinking and the first signs of the search for unity, first within the Churches, and then between them. Let us point to some of the markers in this pioneer age, which were followed in the middle of the twentieth century by the wave of ecumenism.

1. The age of the pioneers

The first signs of the new trend were seen inside the Churches themselves. In the Protestant world, in various countries where missionary societies had first been set up, large world 'Alliances' appeared, created by the Evangelicals (1845), Lutherans (1868), Presbyterians (1877), and Methodists (1881). In 1895, John Mott, the American Methodist, who was to be one of the pioneers of

23

the Ecumenical Movement, founded the World Federation of the Christian Associations of Students.

Within the Anglican Communion, the first Lambeth Conference, called by Dr Longley, the Archbishop of Canterbury, and held in London in 1867, was the earnest of a great future. From 1878, this meeting of all the bishops of the Anglican Communion would be repeated every 10 years. In 1920, the Anglican bishops published an appeal to all Christians for a universal communion on the basis of the Lambeth quadrilateral: the Bible, the Creeds, the Sacraments and the historic Episcopate.

Between the Churches, one meeting was notable, the chance meeting at Madeira in 1889 between the Anglican, Lord Halifax and the Catholic, Fernand Portal. This was to be followed by a spate of initiatives, with new ideas such as the adherence of the Anglican Church as a body to that of Rome. However, this was going too fast and in 1896 hopes were thwarted by the decision of Rome denying the validity of Anglican orders. However, the first step had been taken, and the same trend was to reappear a quarter of a century later during the famous Malines talks, centred around the same protagonists and Cardinal Mercier. After the fifth talk, a report was issued entitled, "The Anglican Church, united not absorbed". However, the time was not ripe for the Catholic Church to free itself of the idea of unity by absorption, and the talks were broken off. Yet, the seed which had been sown would germinate later.

On the Orthodox side, in 1902, the Patriarch of Constantinople, Joachim III, published an ecumenical encyclical. He called on the Orthodox Churches in various countries to strengthen their links with one another, while reaching out to other Churches. Little came of this initiative, so he wrote another letter on the subject in 1904. In 1920, the same Patriarch of Constantinople was to write, this time to *all* Christian Churches, suggesting 11 ways of meeting and working together, including a common calendar, regular reports and the impartial examination of difficulties.[1]

These were just the preliminaries, however, for one date was to become symbolic. In 1910, at the first World Conference of Protestant Missionaries in Edinburgh, a delegate from Africa made such a powerful appeal that a movement was started which could not be stopped. It is still worth pondering the substance of his statement:

You have sent us missionaries, who have taught us to know Jesus Christ, and we thank you. But you have also brought us your distinctions and divisions: some preach Methodism, others Lutheranism, Congregationalism or Episcopalianism. We ask you to preach the Gospel and to let Jesus Christ himself create, among our peoples and with the help of the Holy Spirit, the Church that answers his requirements and responds to the Spirit of our race. This will be the Church of Christ... freed from all the 'isms' from which your teaching of the Gospel among us suffers.[2]

The time was now ripe for this idea to take root and produce practical results. Within Protestantism, two movements, reflecting two complementary insights, were to emerge and develop.

The first was "Life and Work" which, eschewing problems of doctrine, called on Christians to work together in practical, educational, social work, in which everybody could co-operate without difficulty. This would be one way of progressing towards unity – "doctrine divides us," they said, "but action unites us." Nathan Söderblom, the Lutheran Archbishop of Uppsala, was the pioneer here. This initiative resulted in a big congress in Stockholm in 1925.

As a counterpoint to this, another movement arose, "Faith and Order", which chose to work for unity by first tackling the problems of doctrine and theology, which were the cause of the divisions of Christianity. The American Episcopalian bishop, Charles Brent, was the chief protagonist of this. The first congress of this movement was held at Lausanne in 1927.

Meanwhile, what was happening in the Catholic Church? Largely uninvolved with M. Portal's first contacts with Anglicanism, the Church was watching and mistrustful. It did not hide its hostility to "Life and Work", which seemed to make light of the serious problems that divided the Churches. The encyclical *Mortalium Animos* (1928) condemned this new ecumenism shortly after the "Faith and Order" meeting at Lausanne, before there was time to appreciate its significance. The theology of a pure and simple 'return' to the Church continued to prevail.

However, during these same years, some signs of a new attitude appeared. This was first in reference to the East. In 1924, Pope Pius XI wrote to the General of the Benedictine Order, expressing his wish that in each country there should be a monastery especially devoted to work for unity, particularly with the East. In 1926 Lambert Beauduin, who had been behind the letter, founded such a monastery in Belgium, soon to be located at Chevetogne and destined for a great ecumenical future. In 1927, talking to Italian academics, the same Pius XI used beautiful imagery describing the Easterners as "pieces broken from a gold-bearing rock [who] also contain gold. The old Christian regions of the East retain such true holiness that they deserve not merely our respect but all our good will and affection."[3]

In the same year, Catholic, Protestant and Orthodox personnel of a French university, founded a new movement, "Friendship". It was run by a team of laypeople from these Churches, with the aim of knowing and understanding one another better, and working, in honesty and prayer towards the unity of Christians. Later, they adopted Abbot Couturier's formula, and when speaking of the unity to which they aspired, added, "When God wills and as God wills."

The time was coming when attitudes would really change and the concept of unity only as the result of 'absorption' would give way to that of a more mysterious unity. It was around 1937 that the ecumenical movement took root in the Catholic Church. In 1935 and 1937 Abbot Couturier wrote his two articles in *Revue apologétique* which revealed his insights;[4] and in 1937, Father Congar published his book: *Chrétiens désunis: principes d'un oecuménisme catholique*. According to Étienne Fouilloux, the historian of Catholic ecumenism, the former contributed the spirituality, the latter the theology.

The union of the two created a new attitude which Fouilloux finely analyses, using Congar's language. This attitude includes *irenicism* (accepting everything that is love and charity, rejecting anything that is resentful aggressive or irritating, seeking that which is disinterested and brotherly) and *honesty* (rejecting compromise, smartness, dissimulation, and being simple, open, sincere). There is also a real theology of catholicity, although the existing condition of separation means that catholicity is still imperfect... there are merits peculiar to other Christian confessions... Anti-Protestant polemics have caused a certain lack of balance in the Catholic Church.[5]

Naturally, all this did not come about without difficulty. Abbot Couturier was criticized on the ground that his formula was ambiguous.[6] The word 'ecumenism' was still not well regarded in Rome or in many Catholic circles.

In the years before the Second World War, we are still in the pioneer period. But after the war, ecumenism made itself felt and the middle of the century marks the real turning point. In 1948, delayed by the war, the Amsterdam Assembly set up the World Council of Churches (WCC). This linked the two Protestant movements, "Life and Work" and "Faith and Order" whose insights were not contradictory but complementary.

In 1947, the Church of South India emerged, a union of the Anglican Church, the Methodist Church and the United Presbyterian and Congregationalist Church. It recognized existing ministries, but laid down the principle that new ministers should be ordained according to the Anglican Episcopal tradition. In like manner, the Church of North India was founded in 1970.

27

At a more modest level, Brother Roger Schutz, due to the misfortunes of war, settled at Taizé in 1940. He set up a monastic community there in 1949, and wrote their Rule in 1952. As Pastor Boegner was to say a little later, Taizé is "one of the high places of French and World Protestantism, notwithstanding criticism and disparagement, and above all a sign of the yearning for unity which affects a growing number of Christians who want more than anything to be *Christians*. Taizé to some extent at least is a foretaste of restored unity."[7] Then in 1959, Pope John XXIII announced in Rome his decision to call a Council which would be concerned with unity and make many changes.

2. The World Council of Churches (WCC), a ship on an uncharted sea

It took some tenacious men, mainly Protestants, but also Anglicans and the Orthodox, to launch the extraordinary enterprise of bringing together, in an ardent search for unity, ever growing numbers of representatives from all Churches and countries. An exceptional man, Dr Visser't Hooft, was at the centre of these initiatives. Now that the cause is won, we should re-read his humorous description of the awkwardness of the first Assembly, written whilst he was Secretary of this new institution:

> The World Council of Churches is like a newly launched ship about to set off on its first long-haul voyage. This is a unique ship, of an entirely new design, steered by inexperienced officers in charge of a crew not yet fully trained. The officers and the sailors speak different languages and none can understand the other. This vessel sails forth on a stormy night towards an unknown destination, its chosen itinerary uncharted, and a number of journalists have come on board.[8]

All the Churches were invited to Amsterdam, but the WCC made it clear from the start that it had no intention of being some kind of 'super-Church'. It would be no more than a means of bringing people together, a meeting place for listening to what the Spirit would say to the Churches. It merely asked its members to subscribe to a deliberately wide 'base', the WCC being "a fellowship of Churches which accept our Lord Jesus Christ as God and Saviour."

Of the 149 Churches gathered in Amsterdam, the majority were Protestant and Anglican. The Orthodox Church approached on tip-toe, wondering how as an 'apostolic' Church, it would be able to co-exist, undamaged and unconfused, with those Churches whose bishops were not successors of the apostles. The question was not resolved until two years later at the meeting of the Central Committee of the WCC in Toronto, where it was stated unambiguously that each member-Church would retain its own conception of the Church and bear witness to it, whilst respecting the ecclesiological conceptions of the others.

Two absences were striking: the Catholic Church which, having declined the invitation, refused even to send observers; and certain fundamentalist Churches descended from the Reformation with their narrow literal view of the Bible. These Churches went as far as meeting amongst themselves in Amsterdam, one week before the Assembly, in order to denounce the corrupting Catholic influence of the WCC, with its "anti-biblical, anti-evangelical and non-Protestant character".[9]

In spite of the obstacles, the first Assembly was a success and the Christian quality of those responsible for the WCC was clear. Abandoning its initial reservations, the Catholic Church voiced a positive judgement in a document of the Holy Office in 1949 which, whilst not naming the new institution directly, nevertheless recognized ecumenism as an imperative, a reality not without inspiration from the Holy Spirit. The same document gave directives about the manner in which Catholics ought to engage in a dialogue with their brethren from other Churches.[10] The first step was thus taken.

From the beginning, the World Council of Churches built its structures around its Secretary General based in Geneva, Switzerland. *The General Assembly* meet every seven or eight years, each time in a different country with the task of setting out broad outlines. The six members of *The Presidential College*, chosen from different Churches, have overall responsibility. And the *Central Committee* meet annually to decide on how to implement the general directives. Its membership has grown steadily to 150, achieving a fair and almost proportional representation of the various Churches. An imposing 'mechanism' also exists around three large work areas: *Faith and Witness* (the most important element of which is the section "Faith and Order"), *Justice and Service* along the lines of "Life and Work", and *Education and Development*.

Let us pause for a moment to examine the third Assembly, held in New Delhi, India, in 1961, which was

---

ASSEMBLIES OF THE WCC

1984	Amsterdam (Netherlands) *Human disorders and God's plan*	149 Churches
1954	Evanston (USA) *Christ, hope of the world*	163 Churches
1961	New Delhi (India) *Christ, light of the world*	198 Churches
1968	Uppsala (Sweden) *"Behold, I come to make all things new"*	230 Churches
1975	Nairobi (Kenya) *In Christ free and united*	271 Churches
1983	Vancouver (Canada) *Jesus Christ, the way for the world*	304 Churches
1991	Canberra (Australia) *Come Holy Spirit, renew all creation*	317 Churches

important on several counts. First, a new 'base' was adopted. From this point on, the WCC came to be defined as a "Fellowship of Churches which confess our Lord Jesus Christ, God and Saviour, according to the Scriptures, and who strive to respond together to their joint vocation for the glory of the only God, Father, Son and Holy Spirit."

Second, the International Missionary Council (officially founded in 1921 to succeed the International Missionary Conference) joined the Council, as "Faith and Order" and "Life and Work" had from the start, thus bringing into the Council three great worldwide Protestant movements.

Also, the Assembly saw the massive joining up of the Orthodox from Eastern bloc countries (Russia, Romania, Bulgaria and Poland) welcomed by an almost unanimous vote in the Assembly. The Orthodox formed a quarter of the membership of the WCC which thus came to benefit from a better balance of Christian families.

Finally, the Catholic Church was no longer totally absent. For the first time, it sent five official observers and from then on the contacts became more frequent and intense. At the next Assembly, in Uppsala, Sweden, there were 25 observers, bearers of a papal message, and two Catholic speakers addressed the Assembly.

What has happened since? Following the seventh Assembly, held in Canberra in Australia in February 1991, can we make an assessment of the Council, now over 40 years old? First, it seems fit to acknowledge the global success of the WCC unreservedly. When viewed on a historical scale the achievement is prodigious. Less than half a century after the founding of the WCC, most non-Catholic Churches find themselves within it. The number of member-Churches now stands at 317. Only a small number of Evangelical and Pentecostal Churches have remained apart.

There are problems of course. First, there is the tension within the WCC itself, between the 'Protestant' trends and those corresponding to what might be called a 'Catholic' or 'Orthodox' conception. Then, there are other more subtle tensions. These are between the more 'horizontal' trends and those with a more 'vertical' leaning, where the Protestants with an evangelical disposition find themselves close to the Orthodox. Yet, there is another issue which goes deeper than all these. This is the question of the evolution of the WCC which, in spite of its initial determination not to become a 'super-Church,' is moving imperceptibly towards 'ecclesializing' itself in some way. Was not one of the resolutions of the Assembly of Vancouver in 1983 to "undertake a conciliar process of mutual involvement (alliance) in the name of justice, peace and the integrity of all of creation"?[11] It is a known fact that the Orthodox Church as well as the Catholic Church reacted to the ambiguity of the term 'conciliar'. A second problem concerns the non-participation of the Catholic Church. It crops up alongside further questions, trying the patience of some ecumenists to breaking point.

3. The Catholic Church enters the field of ecumenism

In 1928, when the ecumenical movement was still in its early days, the Catholic Church was bluntly stand-offish towards it; but in 1949, after Amsterdam, the reaction was positive. However, it was only with the utmost caution that the Catholic Church took part in the WCC. The Second Vatican Council took a decisive step in 1964 by acknowledging ecumenism to be a valid task for the Church to deal with. In 1976, Pope Paul VI was to go so far as to declare it to be "the most awesome and weighty of (his) pontificate."[12]

The fact a council was called at all had ecumenical implications. Observers from every Church were invited. This went along with a new attitude, getting rid of triumphalism and asking forgiveness for the sins against unity that Catholics may have committed.[13] The adoption of important standpoints was to have considerable consequences for ecumenism.

First came the statement of "a need for a lasting reform of the Church".[14] The entire period of the Council was to be concerned with this need. The *Declaration on Religious Freedom* was one of the most impressive manifestations of this will for renewal and had considerable consequences for ecumenism. Some 20 years later, at the time of the extraordinary Synod in Rome, Cardinal Garonne strongly emphasized this in his masterly inaugural report concerning religious freedom:

> the Council... wanted to lance an abscess. This fine conciliar document, after having been so earnestly debated and finally adopted, ended any painful misunderstanding... it was right to admit that in this sphere mistakes had been made. The document from the Council is a liberating one.[15]

The application of this principle of freedom for couples who contract a mixed marriage was decisive for ecumenism, as will be seen later.

Second, the Council bravely clarified the bond between Christ and the Catholic and other Churches. The way things came about is instructive. A first draft on the *Constitution on the Church* began by giving the ideal definition of what the Church ought to be and then proclaimed that this Church, which Christ wanted *is* the Catholic Church. However, the Council Fathers did not accept this identification of the Church with the model set up and replaced the word 'is' by the formula 'subsists in' *(substitit in)*. The meaning is very clear, while being convinced of the deep faithfulness to Christ, the Church nevertheless does not intend to affirm its correspondence with the ideal definition. It is, as the text insists, "at one and the same time holy and always in need of cleansing".[16]

Along with this, the same document asserts that "a great number of elements of sanctification and truth" are to be found outside the Catholic Church. These elements would be listed in the *Decree on ecumenism*, but with the differences noted, bound up as they are with "the nature and gravity of questions to do with faith and the structure of a Church." There was a real closeness to the Eastern Churches, but there were more serious differences with the Churches and communities separated from the West. The Anglican Communion was a special case (nos. 13-23).

Many other instances could be cited. For example, the need for a change of heart, which is essential for ecumenism (no. 7). A far-reaching event for ecumenism was the assertion (no. 11) that not every doctrinal point in the Catholic Church is to be placed on the same level: "There is an order of 'hierarchy' of truth in Catholic teaching, by reason of their differing relationships to the fundamentals of Christian faith."

In 1965, the *Constitution on revelation* was put to the vote, three years after the definitive rejection of the theory of 'two sources' of revelation – Scripture and Tradition. The existence of *a single source, the Word of God*, was proclaimed (no. 10). This took place on 20 November 1962, and Father Rouquette, reporting in *Études*, suggested that this date should be noted symbolically as the end of the Counter Reformation.[17]

Finally, the Council was in favour of encouraging *ecumenical action*: prayer in common, mutual acquaintance, dialogue and collaboration for concerted activity (no. 12). The decree ended with an invitation to forge ahead. After urging the faithful to avoid both half-heartedness and imprudent zeal, it stressed that "it ardently desires that the initiatives taken by the children of the Catholic Church should make progress and be united with those taken by the separated brethren, without putting any obstacle in the path of Providence and without attempting to forestall the future promptings of the Holy Spirit" (no. 24).

When, at the end of the last session, he said farewell to the observers from other Churches, Pope Paul VI set the tone of the new attitude of the Catholic Church. He said, "We have come to know you a little better... we have acknowledged having made certain mistakes... our Council itself has started to move towards you in many respects... we have begun again to love each other." Recalling that the Catholic Church is aware that it has not betrayed the deposit of faith, and that it has found "treasures of truth and life that it would be impious to give up," he concluded with these bold words: "Reflect that we are all ruled and set free by truth and that truth is near, very near to love."[18] Eventually, action was to reinforce these words.

In 1965, Pope Paul VI and Patriarch Athenagoras lifted the anathemas that Rome and Constantinople had hurled at each other in 1064. The two great Church leaders, who had already met in Jerusalem in 1964, visited each other in 1967, Paul VI taking the initiative by going to Istanbul. The year 1965 also saw the creation of a "Mixed Working Group" with the task of formulating the guiding principles and methods for working together. In this same year, the many Catholics who had visited Taizé were admitted to this Protestant community which had been founded in 1949 by Roger Schutz; and in 1966, the first great meeting of young people took place in Taizé.

Also in 1966, Dr Ramsey, then the Archbishop of Canterbury, went to Rome to visit Pope Paul VI who, as if to give a visible sign of the bond with his episcopal ministry, placed his own pastoral ring on his visitor's finger.

Finally, in 1969, on a journey to Geneva, Paul VI visited the World Council of Churches, greeting it as a wonderful Christian movement.

While the Secretariat for Christian Unity was being organized in Rome, the same years saw the birth, almost everywhere, of centres of training, dialogue and meeting.

A chair for ecumenism was created in the Faculty of Theology in Lyon (1965) and the Institute for Higher Ecumenical Studies was set up in the Faculty of Theology in Paris (1968). Also, the Episcopal Communion for Christian Unity had already been working since the Council. It soon extended to mixed committees for dialogue with Protestants (1968), with Anglicans (1970) and with the Orthodox Church (1980).

At the end of this list, one must mention the astonishing gesture from Paul VI regarding Orthodoxy on the tenth anniversary of the raising of the anathemas. It happened in 1975 at the end of a Mass celebrated in the Sistine Chapel; Metropolitan Meliton, the delegate of Dimitrios the Patriarch of Constantinople, handed the Pope a message to which the latter replied in a few words. Then he suddenly knelt before the Metropolitan and kissed his feet. Surprised and moved, the Metropolitan wanted to do the same, but the Pope would not let him.

An allusion was clearly being made to a painful incident in the fifteenth century, when, at the end of the Council of Florence, Joseph II, the Patriarch of Constantinople had been informed that he could not be dispensed from kissing the Pope's feet. He could not consent to do this, wishing only to give a fraternal embrace, which the Pope was unwilling to accept. The significance of this action in 1975 was deeply touching. Dimitrios immediately issued a statement from Constantinople, hailing "this spontaneous act without precedent in the history of the Church". He saw in it "a certain continuity with the Fathers and the bishops of the undivided Church, who became great because of their humility." He concluded, "By this act, our venerable and beloved Brother, the Pope of Rome, has done more than could be expected of a Pope, and has proved to the Church and to the entire world that he is what he can become, the Christian bishop and, above all, the first of Christian bishops, the Pope of Rome, in fact a reconciling and unifying power for the Church and the world."[19]

Having come last to ecumenism, the Catholic Church

became an active participant in it and gave it full support, to the surprise and sometimes the embarrassment of its partners.

NOTES

1. Details in Olivier Clément, *Dialogues avec le Patriarche Athénagoras*, Fayard 1969, pp. 316-320.
2. Quoted by Suzanne Martineau, *Pédagogie de l'oecuménisme*, Fayard-Mame 1965, p. 268.
3. Quoted by Congar, *Chrétiens désunis: principes d'un oecuménisme catholique*, p. 304.
4. Paul Couturier, "Psychology of the Octave of Prayer from 18 to 25 January", *Revue apologétique*, December 1935; "The universal prayer of Christ for Christian unity", *Revue apologétique*, November-December 1937.
5. Étienne Fouilloux, *Les catholiques et l'unité chrétienne du XIXᵉ au XXᵉ siècle*, Centurion, 1982, pp. 249ff.
6. Even before the start of the Council, the formula was criticized by both theologians and bishops, in the name of the needed 'return'. Cf my article "The Abbé Couturier's prayer for unity" in *Unité Chrétienne*, May 1982, p. 21. However, it was used by Pope John Paul II on the occasion of the ecumenical encounter at Lyons in 1986 (*DC*, 2 November 1986, p. 939).
7. Pastor Marc Boregner, *L'Exigence oecuménique: souvenirs et perspectives*, Aubin Michel, 1968, p. 324. On Taizé, see the "Short History of Taizé," at the end of the pamphlet by Brother Roger, *Son amour est un feu*, Presses de Taizé, 1968. In 1990, the community celebrated the fiftieth anniversary of the arrival in Taizé of Roger Schutz.
8. *La signification ecclésiologique du Concil oecumenique des Églises* by Bruno Chenu, 1945-1963, Beauchesne 1972, p. 368, note 105.
9. Bruno Chenu, op. cit., p. 55.
10. The Instruction *Ecclesia Catholica*, from the Sacred Congregation of the Holy Office, addressed to the bishops of the world, on the "Ecumenical movement," on 20 December 1949 (*DC* 12 March 1950).
11. *Rassemblés pour la vie: rapport officiel de la sixieme assemblée du COE*, published under the direction of Jean-Marc Chapuis and René Beaupère, COE, p. 203. La 7° Assemblée a continué de s'intéresser à ce probleme. Cf. *Signes de l'Esprit. Rapport officiel de la septième Assemblée* publié sous la direction de Marthe Westphal, WCC Publications, Genève, 1991, pp. 14ss.
Cette 7° Assemblée a été l'occasion de soulever des problèmes de fond. Cf notre article: "Le Conseil oecuménique à un tournant", dens *Etudes* juni 1992.
12. Address to the full assembly of the Office for Christian Unity, in 1976, *DC*, 6 February 1977, p. 141.
13. *Decree on ecumenism*, no. 7. Paul VI often treated the theme of repent-

ance (cf *DC* of 3 November 1963, col. 1422; of 12 December 1965, col. 216; of 4 January 1976, p. 27, etc.). Likewise John Paul II (cf *DC*, 21 December 1980, p. 1146; 15 July 1984, p. 705).

14. *Decree on ecumenism*, no. 6.
15. "Retrouver l'élan initial et la grâce du concile", report by Cardinal Garonne, in *DC*, 5 January 1986, pp. 29-30.
16. *Constitution on the Church*, no. 8.
17. *Études*, January 1963, p. 104.
18. *DC,* 19 December 1965, col. 2160-2162.
19. *DC*, 4 January 1976, p. 27.

Chapter 3

The two forces of the ecumenical movement

TOWARDS the middle of the twentieth century, the ecumenical movement compelled recognition from the Churches and became truly irreversible. The initiatives which had been discreetly taking root everywhere began to bear fruit.[1] The seeds of this phenomenon were often sown during the Unity Week gatherings (18-25 January) which provided the opportunity for coming together and which were often the occasion of the start of the first inter-confessional groups. The 'week' was an occasion for organized gatherings, but above all for prayer vigils, based on a theme set out in the tracts of Abbé Couturier to present at parish level the deliberations of the Council of Churches.

This spiritual dimension of ecumenism was essential. Abbé Couturier had already launched the idea of the 'invisible monastery' comprising Christians of all the Churches, unknown to each other, praying for unity. Visible spiritual manifestations of this inspiration were soon to be realized in the two Swiss 'monastic' groups whose communities (Protestant deaconesses and Catholic sisters) have been mixed at Romainmôtres since 1973 and Étoy from 1978 to 1992. As was to be expected, many Catholic convents as well as the new Protestant foundations like the one in Pomeyrol near Tarascon and the deaconesses of Reuilly were to participate in this ecumenical prayer.

Whenever several Churches were present under one roof, a common pastoral ministry sprang up not only in the mixed foyers of the parish but in the field of tourism, in the visits between twinned towns, in media broadcasts and in the trips organized for discovering together other Churches.

FINDING EACH OTHER IN THE
HEART OF CHRIST

The only favourable climate for Christian unity can be found in the prayer of Christ (John 17), or in the agony which prolonged it. Where the heart of Christ prays Christians must search to meet each other. In the prayer of Christ which sanctifies our prayer an exchange takes place: the Father receives my separated brother's prayer of which I am the grateful beneficiary and likewise he welcomes mine, through which my separated brother is enriched. At this level, my brother and I hope for one and the same thing: the unity which Christ desires at the time and by the means that he has ordained. We do not presume to present him with schemes and plans (although we keep our faith intact): we are simply opening our souls before him to accept the fulness of his grace... Let all Christians, wrote Abbé Couturier, draw near to Christ their Lord, with souls open and attentive to the divine invitation, humbly surrendering, as did the humble Virgin Mary. Her reply to the angel is the archetypal utterance of the creature to the creator: "Behold the handmaid of the Lord, be it done unto me according to thy word."

Tract of Unity Week 1955

Pastors and priests would also get together regularly to study the Bible texts on which they would base their homilies.

Progress was also made at the highest level in the field of doctrine and of common action. These are, in effect, the two great bases which the ecumenical movement, since its inception, had intuitively perceived as essential: dialogue in matters of doctrine and common service in the world.

These two currents often drift too far apart when they are propelled by Christians who do not know each other well yet think they are of the same mind; in fact they are destined to be complementary, all Christians being called to use their gifts in the service of doctrine and practice. Let us examine them in turn.

The doctrinal dialogue

One of the most impressive manifestations of the new era in the search for unity has been the unexpected rise and profusion of great doctrinal dialogues. In the past, forerunners like the members of the Dombes Group met, but these were discreet and unofficial. Now, the Churches themselves were taking the initiatives and the World Council of Churches too had launched itself on the journey with its "Faith and Constitution". These various dialogues moved forward together, they were not conducted separately from each other and the exchanges between them were ongoing.

The phenomenon had begun towards the end of the 60's with 'bilateral dialogues'. The Catholic Church had taken several initiatives but, through a dense network, the movement extended to the whole assembly of Churches. On the wider plane, "Faith and Constitution" beat the odds by promoting a 'summit' dialogue among all the Churches, the Catholic Church being officially represented through theologians appointed by Rome.

In the field of bilateral dialogues at the general level, the Catholic Church became involved in ten such dialogues:

1. with the Orthodox Church (1967: "dialogue on charity"; 1975: "theological dialogue")
2. with the Coptic Church (1973)
3. with the Anglican Communion (since 1966)
4. with the World Lutheran Federation (1967)
5. with the World Reformation Alliance (1970)
6. with the World Methodist Council (1967)

7. with the Disciples of Christ (1977)
8. with the World Baptist Alliance (1984)
9. with the Pentecostal groups (1971)
10. with the Evangelicals (1977)

We shall return to these bilateral dialogues when we examine the great living Churches of today.

Let us just pause to look at two very different dialogues which have been in existence for several decades and which have issued definitive documents. The findings of the Dombes Group, a small group which offers the experience of half a century of dialogue; and the dialogue, which has resulted in the issue of a document on Baptism, the Eucharist and the Ministry, currently known as *BEM* which contains contributions from theologians of all the Churches. (These dialogues are uniquely French in character and origin, yet they exemplify the delicate process of ecumenical understanding throughout the worldwide Church.)

The Dombes Group: a precursor

To place the Dombes Group correctly, both in time and space, we should start by saying that it held its first meeting in 1937 at the Cistercian house in Dombes, about 40 kilometres north of Lyons. How did it come about?

Protestant pastors from Switzerland decided to invite Abbé Remillieux, a priest from Lyon and a friend of Abbé Paul Couturier, to join them for their pastoral meeting. Once Abbé Couturier had heard the enthusiastic account of the time they had spent with the pastors, he sensed instinctively what should happen. Priests and pastors needed to spend a few days together, in an atmosphere of brotherly love, so that they could get to know one another, pray together, and really begin to understand what was separating them. The eventual hope was to rebuild the unity which had been lost. Although this idea might seem commonplace to us today, it was unheard of at that time.

In this way, therefore, a group was formed which had no specific definition or precise rules, and was able to work and evolve in complete freedom. It consisted of equal numbers of Catholics and Protestants (currently 20 of each, which include a number of Swiss as well as French members). There was only one firmly agreed element: an annual reunion would be held during the first week of September. This would be hosted alternately by a Catholic house and by a Protestant house in either France or Switzerland. However after 1972, the Group decided for logistical reasons to meet permanently at Dombes, which had initially been suggested to Abbé Couturier by his bishop, Cardinal Gerlier – whence its name.

The Group had no official mandate from the Churches, and was therefore able to determine its own course of action with complete independence. There was only one aspect which called for some caution, and that was the care needed in the actual choice of pastors and priests, so as to ensure that they were truly representative of the Churches in which they exercised their ministry with the full backing of their bishops and synods. It was this two-fold guarantee of freedom of investigation on the one hand, and of the ecclesiastical qualifications of the members on the other, which gave a real moral authority to the Group and transformed its statements into classic reference documents.

One characteristic of the Group from the beginning, was that its free and open discussions were based on three closely interlinked parts: *theological investigation* (which first had to feel its way, but soon began to concentrate on the major themes); a climate in which *genuine dialogue* could exist (this was greatly facilitated by the members' deep mutual understanding, as the participation of everyone had been regular and consistent); and *an atmosphere of prayer* ("a theology which was streaming with prayer", as Abbé Couturier used to say). All of this did not evolve from some sort of elaborate protocol but was accomplished empirically, purely through the initiative of individuals. In essence, dialogue was learned experimentally by listening

43

to those of true dialogue next to whom those of monologue soon became unbearable!

For many years the Group 'produced' nothing. It was simply a place for meeting, and for the ecumenical growth of the participants. However, after some 20 years of familiarization, the custom grew of drafting short commentaries on the experiences of each session. This was only done if it were appropriate, and then just for the participants' own use. It was not until 1966, 30 years after the first meeting, that the time seemed right to begin to publish these. In any event, it was in response to an expectation, and to a very specific demand, which resulted from the first major youth gathering at Taizé, on the eve of the Dombes Group meeting, that the in-depth study on the Eucharist was begun.

If the dialogue at Dombes was from many points of view exemplary, the reason for this was simply that it gave itself plenty of time. Gradually and progressively, the Group absorbed the progress it made into its collective memory, and this ensured that it was consistent, both in its method of working and in its ability to position itself. In this way the Group could recall, after the event, the very moment when they found themselves no longer gazing at each other *face to face*, full of goodwill and searching for mutual understanding, but suddenly *side by side*, engaged in a common search. (They fixed the symbolic date of 1956 for this event.) Solid experience of true dialogue is infectious, and after many years of involvement in the Group, I myself can testify to this.

Let us now try to highlight some of the experiences which marked their progress. One of the first benefits was to strip away the mystery from the pitfalls of vocabulary. In order to describe one and the same reality Protestants used certain words and Catholics others, and each filled the other with fear. On the subject of the Eucharist, for example, Protestants spoke of 'memorial' and Catholics of 'sacrifice'. In consequence, the unwary Catholic concluded instinctively that the Protestant Eucharist was an insubstantial evocation ("it's not hard to see that the Real Presence doesn't exist for them!"); while the Protestant immediately thought, "Typical of the Catholics! The sacrifice of Christ himself isn't enough for them, and they take it upon themselves to add their own little personal sacrifices to it!" It is true that an indifferent Catholic or Protestant catechism could lead to a belief in some form of watered-down Protestant memorial and to Catholic sacrifices which were simply added on like carriages to a train. However, the relaxed dialogue enabled the participants in the Dombes Group to understand that the Protestants who were there used the word 'memorial' in the strong sense (i.e. as the Memorial of Easter celebrated the Lord who is the same yesterday and today and who saves his people). Also, for the Catholics who were there, the Mass was not some sort of supererogatory sacrifice, but was the real enactment of Christ's unique and wholly sufficient sacrifice. Once this was thoroughly understood, it soon became clear that, even using different words, the meaning was essentially the same – at least in the simplest cases, as different Protestant traditions do not always use the same language.

These conscientious struggles were sometimes facilitated by clarification from a theologian of a different Church. Although the Group consisted of Catholics and Protestants – and this initial choice was never in question – it frequently had access to Orthodox or Anglican experts. In 1967, for example, Paul Evdokimov came to speak to the Group on the subject of the Eucharist in the Orthodox Church. Having clarified to the Catholics that they could accept the validity of his own Eucharist, he went on to astonish many of them by recalling that there were nevertheless major differences between the two Churches. For example, the Orthodox Church never used the word 'transubstantiation', which was essentially part of the vocabulary of Western scholastics from the Middle Ages and was not understood by either Russians or Greeks. Moreover, the Orthodox Church did not reserve the Eucharist in the tabernacle. Conversely, Protestants discovered that those elements of Catholic vocabulary and practice which had given them so much difficulty did not in fact exist in a Church whose Eucharist was totally recognized and accepted by Catholics. Four years later, the conclusions of the Group on the subject of the Eucharist were to show clearly these influences.

The study of Scripture was of course always at the centre of the Group's meditations, the Word of God being the communal treasure which was their starting point. Yet, the Group quickly came to realize how much the views of both denominations had been conditioned by the interpretations traditionally held by each Church. Some aspects of which had become firmly set after centuries of dispute. The result was that, before even opening the Bible, they had to start by asking themselves how Holy Scripture had been read and understood during the first millennium by Christians in a Church which was still undivided. Then they compared these 'communal' interpretations – with all their diversity and differences – with the 'conflictual' readings and interpretations of the second millennium. This approach was applied rigorously in the last two published statements of the Group, and resulted in some fascinating struggles of conscience.

One of the determining attitudes of the Group was that these struggles of theological conscience should not become entrenched and re-positioned as central intellectual disputes, but should resonate through the life of the Churches. In each of the statements, therefore, the theological element was backed up by a pastoral element, given in the form of 'recommendations' to the Churches. These applied both to the area of language as well as sacramental or community aspects. Indeed, following an exposition of the respective temptations of the Group, these recommendations were essentially an appeal for ecclesiastical *metanoia*. For example, the Catholic tendency to reproduce in local Church structures levels of tremendous centralization comparable with those of the universal Church, and the Protestant temptation to settle simply for spiritual unity in the universal Church, were both condemned equally.

Interestingly, the conflict of differing opinions, or sometimes simply lone voices, often opened up the way to complementary points of view. For example, what do Protestants and Catholics conceive to be the true and authentic road of apostolic succession? For Catholics, the element which has spontaneously taken precedence is the historical and authoritative succession of the bishops of the Church (putting undue stress, therefore, on the mechanical process of ordination, without concern for its expression both in faith and in life). For Protestants, the most essential element was fidelity both in faith and in life (so paying insufficient attention to the laying on of hands and the ministry which resulted from this). A quotation from St Irenaeus, brought up at a timely moment by historians from both Churches, reminded each of them of some important facts. They needed to hold to the idea of *the apostolic succession of the whole Church* (whereby all the faithful must cling to the faith of the apostles and imitate the life of the apostles). They must also hold to the belief in *the apostolic succession in ministry* (symbolized by the laying on of hands on certain individuals only, to confer special responsibilities on them). The particular recommendations for each Church evolved naturally and easily from this.

In conclusion, the predominant theme of the long road which the Dombes Group has travelled is a call for the conversion of the Churches, and this has been reiterated in every statement. However, it was never conceived as a conversion which would involve the loss of the individual identity of any Church. The Group completed its sixth statement in September 1990, the title of which sums this up, *Pour la conversion des Églises: identité et changement dans la dynamique de conversion* (For the conversion of the Churches: identity and change in the dynamic of conversion).

An important first: the BEM Document

The Document entitled "Baptism, Eucharist, Ministry," – generally called *BEM* – came into being in 1982 in Lima, Peru, during the plenary assembly of the commission on "Faith and Constitution". This was at the end of a long period of preparation, for the idea of the research had first been adopted in 1927 at a meeting of the same commission in Bristol. The work, originally confined to the Eucharist, was later expanded to include Baptism and the Ministry. The result was a small volume of less than 100 pages in three parts.[2] Each of these three entities is described by the features accepted by the different Churches, pointing out, when the need arises, the divergencies of opinion. After this statement of facts, which allows all parties to get to know each other better and to discover that sometimes their differences are not so marked as they had imagined, there follow some remarks, explanations and additional material which seek unity.

Thus, *BEM* is original in several ways. First, it is the work of representatives of most of the Churches, which is without doubt an important factor in the history of the separated Churches. The list of participants speaks volumes. Out of the 128 members present at Lima, 114 were delegates of Churches belonging to the World Council of Churches. They were: 76 Protestants (33 Reformed Protestants, 22 Lutherans, 13 Methodists, 8 Baptists), 23 members of the Orthodox Church, 14 Anglicans, and 1 representative of the Old Catholics. The 14 others belonged to Churches which were not members of the Council: 12 Catholics (theologians appointed by Rome to be an integral part of "Faith and Constitution" since 1968; one of them, Fr Tillard, is even vice-president of this commission), 1 Pentecostal and 1 Adventist.

A second original feature, which has not always been clearly understood, is that this is not an 'agreement', but a 'summary text', to be 'received' after a period of reflection and assimilation. An agreement is the fruit of a unanimous group of authors, which is offered to readers who either accept or reject it. A summary text, on the other hand, is an entity with which, by definition, nobody agrees. It juxtaposes differences of common belief, trying to further mutual knowledge, but with a constant effort to bring people's viewpoints closer together.

Finally, *BEM* is not initially offered to be 'received' by individuals, but by the Churches represented in Lima. What is asked of each Church, therefore, is that it should not slip into an *a priori* reaction of rejection but, on the contrary, allow itself first to be challenged by the description of the positions of the other Churches before, perhaps, distancing itself from them. Put another way, without actually using the word, what is suggested is a real process of *metanoia*. This is certainly the meaning behind the third of the four questions put to the Churches at the beginning of the text, asking what are "the guidelines which your Church can receive from this text concerning its life and witness in the areas of liturgy, education, ethics and spirituality."

Without analysing the content of *BEM*, let us simply say that the consensus among the Churches concerning *Baptism* is very strong. However, the serious problem posed by the demand of the evangelical Churches for baptism by immersion and their rejection of infant baptism must be noted. It is less strong concerning the *Eucharist*, especially when the "Real Presence" in the Eucharist is brought into question, and how the bread and wine left over after the Eucharist should be treated. The most marked differences of opinion are those on the *Ministry*, such as problems of ordination, with the ordination of women occasioning a conflict of opinions which cannot at present be resolved. We should, however, note that above and beyond these diverging opinions about the concept of the ministry, the principle is clearly stated that the ordained ministry is a "constituent part of the life and witness of the Church".[3]

To give a concrete example of the way *BEM* works,

calling readers to reflection and 'conversion,' let us quote just one significant page on the exercise of the ordained ministry. This, it is said, should be exercised in three ways – personal, collegial and communal (no. 26):

> The ordained ministry should be exercised in a *personal* way. A person ordained to proclaim the Gospel and call the community to serve the Lord in unity of life and witness most effectively shows the presence of Christ when in the midst of his people. The ordained ministry should be exercised in a *collegial* way, that is to say, that a college of ordained ministers is needed to share the task of representing the community's concerns. Finally, the close relationship between the ordained ministry and the community should find its expression in a *communal* dimension, that is to say, that the exercise of the ordained ministry must be rooted in the life of the community and that it necessitates a positive participation in seeking the will of God and the guidance of the Spirit.

A commentary on this points out that these three aspects were bound together in the early Church, where there existed at the same time the office of bishop, councils of elders and the role of the community of the faithful. Later, and especially after division set in, some aspects became more important and some other aspects less. In this way, the various systems of ecclesiastical organization appeared: *Episcopalianism*, *Presbyterianism* and *Congregationalism*. Here, authority rested with bishops, synods, or communities of the faithful respectively, each of which was considered essential to the good order of the Church by its adherents. Yet, these three systems should take their place together in the reunified Church. Each Church should be questioned and invited to a conversion, to attain a greater fidelity to the apostolic Church.

2. Common action

Although the common action of Christians as such does not present any dogmatic problem, it was at first viewed with suspicion by the Catholic Church. The reason for this is simple. Certain Protestant voices tended to associate common action with an undervaluing and even distrust of dogmatic dialogue ("doctrine divides, action unites"). Similarly professional theologians scorned this action which appeared to them far removed from the basic problems of disunity. Fr Congar, the great ecumenical theologian, admitted candidly that he remained distrustful for a long time, being too close to scholastic philosophy. "Misled by the rather confined phrasing of certain advocates of practical Christianity," he wrote, "I did not see the deep truth which is revealed by way of joint action."[4]

However, initiatives for common action had started quickly from the grass roots level. The *Decree on ecumenism* encouraged Catholics and specified all the areas in which collaboration with the separated brethren, already under way, "must be stressed without respite". It particularly noted respect for the human person, promotion of peace, the social application of the Gospel, in the development of the sciences and the arts, and in the battle against the misery of our time (hunger, natural disasters, ignorance, poverty, the housing crisis and the unequal distribution of wealth) (no. 12). As this wave of ecumenism spreads, common action increases, becoming more and more inventive. However, it was not always without problems or resistance, because passing from confrontation or competition to collaboration is not decreed by a stroke of the pen nor is it instantly achieved.

Two documents from the "Mixed Working Party"

To clear the way and to encourage effort the "Mixed Working Party" of the Catholic Church and the World

Council of Churches published two documents, which are still interesting to reread.

The first document, published in 1970, is principally concerned with difficulties resulting from two mandates. On the one hand, each Church must preserve the freedom to give witness from its own particular identity. On the other, this witness must not be manifested as proselytizing. The "Mixed Working Party" therefore, proceeded very slowly. This first text, worked out at length by a commission and amended after many consultations, is presented as a "working document" which has not obtained the unanimous support of the people involved but "expresses a large area of agreement" and which is submitted to the Churches for their reflection. The title is evocative, *Common witness and proselytism of the wrong kind*.[5] Given the often ambiguous meaning of the word 'proselytism' in different languages, only proselytism "of the wrong kind" is condemned, "that which violates the right of every human being not to undergo any exterior constraint in religious matters." Or again, "ways of preaching the Gospel which are not conformed to the ways of God and invites man to respond freely" (no. 8). Witness must be "conformed to the spirit of the Gospel and anxious to do nothing to compromise the progress of dialogue and ecumenical action" (no. 25).

Concerning the 'transition' of members from one Church to another in pursuit of religious liberty, one must avoid speaking of 'conversion'. Each Church is invited to exercise great discretion, especially where children and adolescents are concerned. Two instructions are given, "Let the Church that receives a new member be aware of the ecumenical repercussions of this change and not draw from it any vain glory. Let the Church that has been left not conceive any bitterness or rancour and not ostracize the person concerned" (no. 28).

Against the background of a call to loyalty this document opens up a vast area to common witness and common action:

- development of the individual and of the human race;
- defence of the rights of humanity and of religious liberty;
- battle against economic, social and racial injustices;
- the promotion of international understanding, arms limitation, the establishment and preservation of peace;
- the campaign against illiteracy, hunger, alcoholism, prostitution, drugs trafficking;
- the medical and sanitary services, and other social facilities;
- assistance to victims of accidents and natural disasters.

Besides this list oriented towards the world, the document also mentions collaboration between the Churches in the fields of biblical translation, catechesis, education, use of the media, without forgetting the area of prayer, particularly during Unity Week (nos. 14-15).

The second document, which came out 10 years later, is entitled *The common witness of Christians*[6] and is also presented as a working paper. In the meantime, collaboration between the Churches has intensified, "The Holy Spirit, in calling Christians to act together according to their new forms in order to respond to new situations, has also roused the conscience to realize the urgency of common witness" (no. 9). There is a lengthy insistence on the foundation of this witness to the Good News of Jesus Christ and on its source which is the Living Trinity. The list of areas open to common action remains the same, but one notices an insistence on involvement in "problems of social justice, in the name of the poor and oppressed," since the Church is the "mouth and voice of he oppressed in the face of the establishment" (no. 37).

One must not forget the difficulties already discussed, recalling a phrase that proselytism of the wrong kind must be viewed as "an unworthy form of witness" (no. 51). "We do not hide the problems posed by the Churches often maintaining very different positions, especially in the area of ethics, which leads us to emphasize that "a divided witness can become counter-productive" (no. 41).

Finally, the document solemnly recalls the formula created at the meeting of "Faith and Constitution" at Lund in 1952, "inviting all the Churches to do together whatever does not interfere with fidelity to conscience" (no. 40). The Churches therefore can engage, without fear, in common action. In spite of difficulties which arise, as the level of involvement becomes higher and more difficult, they have co-operated with constancy and tenacity.

A few concrete examples

Let us look at a few examples taken from France which highlight Christian responses to persistent social problems. First, there is the peace issue. This was initially taken up in "Some Reflections on the Arms Trade," which was a positive and common stand adopted by the Churches.[7]

Ten years later, however, the media happily exploited two divergent positions, taken within a few days of each other, which differed on the central issue of nuclear deterrents. The first had been that taken at the Catholic Episcopal Conference on 8 November 1983 (*To Win Peace*). While vehemently advocating non-violence, the Conference accepted nuclear disarmament almost unconditionally, as a distressing solution to be discarded as soon as possible.[8] Five days later, on 13 November, the Protestant Federation meeting in La Rochelle composed a short document (*The Fight for Peace*) demanding a nuclear, and even a unilateral, freeze.[9]

Certainly, the hasty drafting of these two documents and their apparent elaboration without any form of dialogue were a cause for concern on the part of members of the various Churches, particularly when it soon became apparent that there was discord at the heart of their Churches. The issue was again raised a month later, on 15 December, at the annual joint meeting of delegates from the two permanent councils, the Catholic and the Reformed Lutheran. They issued a statement immediately acknowledging the basic similarities between the two texts (something which the press paid little attention to, concentrating rather on the differences). They asked followers of the two Churches to read the two documents with a critical and constructive eye and to encourage an even greater awareness of the teachings of the Gospel. It could not have been better expressed, yet there was little in the way of a common, steadfast and positive testimony in response to this pronouncement.[10]

In the years that followed, a variety of groups set about trying to show a common stand on these delicate issues, and two pamphlets were published. In 1985, two French organizations which had already entered into dialogue, the Justice and Peace Commission (Catholic) and the International, Social and Economic Commission (Protestant), issued a joint publication, *Towards building the peace: ecumenical research.* In 1989, a group of Catholics and Protestants (18 national organizations, about 100 smaller groups and associations and a number of individual signatories, including 13 bishops) endorsed a further document, *Another way to fight: towards non-violent, responsible and effective action: Christians speak out.*

Moving on to the issues of family and sexual ethics, events have taken a different course. In December 1981, the permanent Catholic and Reformed Lutheran Councils, realizing the drawbacks of adopting separate positions which were seen by public opinion to be divergent, decided to create a joint *ad hoc* commission to consider these issues. Four Protestants and several Catholics met regularly in the following year to carry out a basic study. The result of their efforts, approved by the authorities who had commissioned the work, was a report which clarified and unveiled the false interpretations of the differences. It pointed out that the theological source of the problem was the Creation and Redemption dichotomy, where the Protestants place great emphasis on a breach and the Catholics, on continuity.[11]

On another occasion a few years later, the joint Catholic-Protestant commission focussed on the more concrete aspects of these ethical questions and together published *Catholics and Protestants and moral doctrine in a secular society*,[12] which was seen as "the first, modest but nevertheless significant, step towards a common policy on ethics, given the new questions of conscience posed by developments in science and technology." Did this mean that a way was being forged across this stony ground, albeit slowly, towards a genuine common stand?

A final case of joint ecumenical action, Christian Action for the Abolition of Torture (CAAT), is indeed an example of success on all sides. There is a close union between all people of goodwill, a specifically Christian dimension and complete, joint ecumenical responsibility.

The idea for Christian action against torture came, in 1974, from several Parisian Protestants who had been much distressed by a lecture given by Pastor Tullio Vinai, who had returned from South Vietnam and revealed the inhuman treatment to which political prisoners were subjected. This group of Protestants decided to make various Christian Churches aware of the problem of torture and their initiative was well received. They contacted Amnesty International, which the previous year had made a specific appeal for the support of the Church in its efforts. It was agreed that the new organization would work closely with Amnesty International, but would remain independent and retain its specifically Christian character. It was from this that CAAT was born, with a Catholic, a Protestant and an Orthodox at the helm. Its aims were as follows:

– to make Christians in particular aware of the horror of torture, without making any distinctions in political regime or country;

– to encourage Christians to use spiritual means, prayer in particular, to bring about the abolition of torture;

– to bring about any form of effective action, be it individual or collective, aimed at the suppression of all forms of torture;

– to work, in this fight, with people of goodwill.[13]

Very soon groups were being formed all over France and these remained interdenominational wherever several different Churches were involved. Several monks and nuns took part, introducing a spiritual dimension with their consecrated prayer. One means of action available to everyone and the effectiveness of which is easily determined is the sending of thousands of letters to individuals within the governments of the various countries, and to the jailers in the prisons and camps where torture is practised, often with the name of a specific prisoner. In 1977, the movement wrote a collective letter to all the world's torturers. In the same year, it sent another letter to the World Council of Churches and to the Pope, both of whom responded favourably.

While action against torture is CAAT's prime concern, all their activities are carried out in an ecumenical manner. The experience has shown that Christians from the various Churches involved are imbued with a common sense of urgency. The overall spirit of their action is evangelical, because "ultimately man is due respect by virtue of his resemblance to God. Through the suffering of Jesus he is the image of God on earth. And Jesus says that his is the destiny of even the meekest of men" (Matthew 25:40,45).[14]

Official meetings of the Churches

Alongside the groups engaged in theological dialogue and those planning common action, the ecumenical movement has given rise to other types of meetings which have an institutional and inter-ecclesiastical status as well as a pastoral aim. Let us consider three examples, at different levels.

At the national level in France, one could begin by mentioning the 'Chantilly' meetings, one of the most original experiments in French ecumenism. These take the form of a large triennial gathering of about 200 people responsible for ecumenism in the Catholic dioceses, in the Protestant regions, and in the Orthodox and Anglican Churches. They meet in the big conference centre after which the meetings are named. This gathering began in Lyon with a meeting of the Catholic representatives. The meeting was then transferred in 1968 to Bièvres, in the Paris region, near another house, Roche-Dieu, where Protestant representatives were meeting, and there was a gradual symbiosis between the two groups. This finally led in 1974 to a fully merged meeting at Chantilly, organized with complete co-responsibility. There for four days, in an atmosphere of fervent prayer, they experienced a profound communion stronger than any division between them. Lectures by experts from the various Churches, discussion groups to assess what was at stake, acts of testimony to deepen consciousness of the issues, free time in which to make more contacts – all make the meetings into a powerful experience for the ecumenical leaders.[15]

Interdenominational meetings between the highest authorities in the various Churches were a more difficult matter. They were reached in two stages. Initially, 18 delegates of the Permanent Council of the French Catholic Episcopal Conference and the Lutheran-Reformed Permanent Council met for a day in December 1980. These bishops, ministers, priests and laypeople discussed pastoral problems common to all the Churches and subjects of contention at that time. This continued each year and the length of the meeting was soon increased by starting on the previous evening.

This originally was a meeting only between Catholics and Protestants. Gradually the idea germinated for a real Council of Churches, including in particular, the Orthodox. These Councils of Churches were not something completely new. They had begun to spring up around the world, gradually and without anyone realizing it, during the 1970s. In 1975, the Catholic Church issued a document on "Ecumenical collaboration at regional, national and local levels"[16] which was devoted mainly to these Councils. It is noticeable that this text is in a distinctly new style. It recognizes current achievements in all their diversity, and gives them general approval without burdening them with premature recommendations. It also insists on the necessary adaptation to local needs, and gives authentic independence to the dioceses and episcopal conferences. Back in 1975, there were 19 of these Councils in which the Catholic Church participated. There are now more than 40. One of the latest to be set up is that of the Near East (January 1990).

The "Council of Christian Churches in France" was born on 17 December 1987 after two years of negotiations and after approval by the authorities of the Churches concerned. Consisting of 18 members, a third from the Catholic Church, a third from the Churches of the Protestant Federation of France and a third from the Oriental Churches (Orthodox and Armenian), the Council has a collegial authority, with a new president each year. Its charter specifies that "the aim at the start is modest but open to the voice of the Spirit" and there is no question of creating a new structure whose authority would in some way be imposed on the member Churches. The Council proposes for itself:

— that it should be a place for *exchange of information, listening* and *dialogue*;

— that it should facilitate *reflection* and, as the occasion arises, *common initiatives* in three areas: Christian presence in society, service and witness.

Still in its first few years, the organization is not yet out of its teething period and we should not expect spectacular results from it too quickly. The main point is that it exists and shows by its very existence that, even when they are separated, the Churches are more and more bound together in a march towards unity which is taking place irreversibly before our eyes – a march which must find its own rhythm.

Let us now go outside the boundaries of France and consider two great gatherings which have taken place recently: in Europe, the meeting in Basle; and at world level, the meeting in Seoul. Both had the same theme, "Justice, Peace and the Integrity of Creation" – a theme which lent itself to the sort of common action which could unite the efforts of all the Churches without any major dogmatic problems. The Catholic Church took part in both, but in different ways. An examination of its respective forms of participation is instructive for understanding what the difficulties were and what was at stake.

The Basle meeting at Whitsun 1989 was in a sense a great first, since it brought together representatives of the Churches of 25 European countries – belonging on the one hand to the World Council of Churches and on the other to the Catholic Church. It was organized in co-operation with neither Rome nor Geneva, but with what could be called two European 'collectives'. The KEK (*Konferenz Europäischer Kirchen* – Conference of European Churches) has included since 1959 all the European Churches belonging to the World Council of Churches and is presided over by Metropolitan Alexis of Leningrad; and the CCEE (*Conseil des Conférences Épiscopales d'Europe* – Council of European Episcopal Conferences) has since 1968 brought together the Catholic Episcopal Conferences and is presided over by Cardinal Martini.

The two bodies had already held four meetings together, hosted alternately by the Catholics and the Protestants (in 1978 at Chantilly, in 1981 at Lögumkloster in Denmark, in 1984 at Riva del Garda and Trent in Italy, and in 1988 at Erfurt in Germany). Well initiated by these years of work together and taken forward by two similarly structured organizations, the Assembly in Basle was a success. Its final document will remain as a reference text translating the unanimous conviction of the Churches into the three closely linked and very important areas of Peace, Justice and the Integrity of Creation. On each of these themes, Christians are obliged not only to work side by side with their fellow human beings, but also to commit themselves as representatives of their faith to God the Creator who is a God of Peace and of Justice. The Orthodox Church, moreover, has just instituted a liturgical Feast of the Creation on the first Sunday of September.

It was rather different at the world assembly in Seoul.[17] The World Council of Churches had wanted the Catholic Church to agree to be a joint host and joint organizer, as it had been at the European meeting in Basle. However, the Catholic Church did not agree to this. For, unlike in Basle, the two organizations would not have been of equivalent standing: on one side there would have been a Church, but on the other, there would have been an organization, the WCC, which as such does not commit its member Churches.[18] Certain members of the WCC perceived clearly that there was a serious risk that this would not work. It is indeed noticeable that the only example of failure in the collaboration between the WCC and the Catholic Church was that of 'Sodepax' – the Commission for Society, Development and Peace. Founded in 1968 with an expectation that there would be joint responsibility and with an aim close to the theme of the assembly in Seoul, this body had an apparently promising start, but never managed to function well and ceased to exist after about 12 years. The fact remains that in Seoul the belated and negative Catholic response was badly received. Nevertheless, even without being a joint organizer, the Catholic Church made its presence felt in Seoul through its theological and even its financial contribution and through its observers, and joined fully in the procedures.

The assembly itself was in many respects a success. It must, however, be stated that, even though its official membership was limited to the delegates of the WCC, its final conclusions were less unanimous than those reached in Basle. The lessons to be drawn from all this are, no doubt, that action in common remains a delicate matter, that meetings on a world level pose specific problems and that, if advances are to be made, the time must be ripe and appropriate terms of operation must be established in advance. The practice of ecumenism requires both patience and impatience!

The ten affirmations of the Seoul assembly

1. We must render an account to God of any exercise of power.
2. God makes an option in favour of the poor.
3. All peoples and all races have equal value.
4. Men and women are created in the image of God.
5. Truth is the basis of a community of free beings.
6. Jesus Christ brings peace.
7. Creation is loved by God.
8. The earth belongs to the Lord.
9. The dignity and the commitment of the young generation must be recognized.
10. Human rights are given by God.

The four commitments of the Seoul assembly

1. To work for the establishment of a just *economic order* and for liberation from slavery of foreign debt.
2. To work for the institution of genuine *security* for all peoples and all nations and a culture of non-violence.
3. To work for the conservation of the earth's environment and for the building of a culture which respects *creation*.
4. To work for the elimination of *racism* and of discrimination against any human beings at any level and also for the elimination of types of behaviour which perpetuate the sin of racism.

3. Between impatience and patience

One of the problems with being on the crest of the ecumenical wave is combining patience with impatience while avoiding the two extremes of too much haste or too much delay. There exists an *evangelical impatience* like that of St Paul, driven by an urgent desire to announce the Good News; and that of the true witnesses of the Gospel throughout the centuries, burning to work for the kingdom of God. There also exists a *totally human impatience*, which seems to believe the achievement of the kingdom will be the result of our current efforts and the conclusion of our own plans!

Conversely, there is an authentic *evangelical patience*, which knows how to await, not without suffering, the moment when the time is ripe. This must be distinguished from a *totally human pseudo-patience*, which in reality is nothing more than a lack of the will (literally 'laziness') to learn and move, a lack of the will to listen to the Spirit.

Working for the unity desired by Christ, in the time-frame and by means that he wishes, requires the joining of evangelical patience with evangelical impatience – and perseverance. Two contrasting examples illustrate this point:

– at the base, the problem of sharing the Eucharist;
– at the summit, the problem of the relations between the Catholic Church and the World Council of Churches.

Sharing the Eucharist

The problem of sharing the Eucharist has been posed most forcefully by couples of mixed marriages, i.e. where the partners belong to two different Churches, usually the Catholic Church and a Reformed or Lutheran Church. We should use these couples as a starting point to understand the urgency of their petitioning.

For a long time mixed marriages, if not prohibited, were at least discouraged by the Churches, for they represented a reality that was almost impossible to live out during the anathema, when unity could only be imagined as the absorption of one Church by another. The solution at that time was for the 'stronger' of the two spouses to draw the other into his or her own Church. For its part, the Catholic Church would require that it conduct the marriage ceremony itself, and would insist on a written commitment, known as a 'caution', from non-Catholic partners, guaranteeing the baptism and instruction of their children in the Catholic Church. Even though they did not require such a precise commitment, the other Churches frequently had a moral equivalent.

Then things changed. In particular, the *Declaration of the Second Vatican Council on religious freedom* led to the end of 'cautions', perceived as a constraint on the freedom of the non-Catholic partner. The latter was simply asked to "do his or her best" so that his or her children might be baptized and raised in the Catholic Church. Also, it was accepted, for pastoral reasons, that the marriage might, on occasion, be celebrated before a non-Catholic minister.[19] It was also agreed on both sides that the Church which celebrated the marriage might make way for some participation by the minister from the other Church. The ceremony became a celebration where everyone could feel at ease. A new process was being started.

The first result, which favoured the growth of ecumenism, was the appearance of a pastoral community of mixed marriages, which had the characteristic of depending on neither of the two Churches individually, but rather on both, even if each partner continued, personally, to belong to his or her own Church. Concerned priests and pastors began to meet to take charge of these thoroughly original families. It was noticed that the spouses, through a sort of spiritual competition, were not forming a 'third church', but were often becoming stronger believers and more active in their own Church, while maintaining a link with the other. In these households, wrote Fr Beaupère, "the conjoined (*conjuncti*) are men and women whose situation calls on them providentially to go beyond the situation of separated brethren (*se-juncti*, according to the wording of Vatican II). They are the *connecting tissue* which, little by little, is bringing together the lips of the wound, healing the injury and bridging the gap of the division between our Churches."[20]

From then on, a new question was posed: was it possible always to stay apart on Sunday mornings, each partner going to services at his or her own Church? In situations where their parish Churches were close, spouses started going to them together from time to time, following the rhythms that seemed appropriate to them, and they felt good in the nourishment of their faith. This could not fail to bring up the question of sharing the Eucharist: was it truly impossible to take communion in the other Church? Partners in mixed marriages were insistent about the problem. Their impatience joined with that of experienced ecumenical groups, who were also requesting the possibility of sharing communion, at least as an exception.

This is a complex problem, for it still depends on the pastoral teaching of the different Churches, who do not all have the same method of solving it, each pointing out that they have their own good reasons. Let us now examine them in some detail.[21]

The Orthodox Church lays special emphasis on the strong link between the Church and the Eucharist. For this Church, participation in the Eucharist is an expression of total communion in the faith. Under these conditions, eucharistic sharing seems to be impossible so long as the Churches are separated. To place the sign of unity where unity does not exist would be acting a lie, all the more serious when it is a question of the Body and Blood of Christ. In practice, the application of the 'principle of economy' – according to which evangelical charity, in a specific case, may lead to a certain relaxation of the rules – may allow a few exceptions, but the rule remains nonetheless strict.

As far as the Reformed Churches are concerned, although there is a certain range of opinion, the general reasoning on the subject is exactly the opposite. Reformed Christians, always anxious not to stress the role of the Church, which they likes to describe as "coming second, though not secondary", consider above all that it is Christ himself who celebrates the Eucharist through his ministers. Therefore it is the Lord who invites us to the eucharistic table. How, then, could we not respond to his invitation, since it is a matter of two Churches which recognize the validity of each other's baptism? In an actual ecumenical situation, if Protestants attend Mass and cannot approach the communion table because the Catholic Church does not invite them to do so, they consider this an anomaly and find it hard to understand, because the eucharistic table of their own Protestant Church is open to all baptized Christians who wish to approach it.

The Catholic Church has yet another position in regard to what it calls the *communicatio in sacris*, that is, participation in prayer, liturgy and above all the eucharistic communion of a Church from which it is separated. In the main, its position is close to that of the Orthodox, but with a little less strictness, which makes it more complicated. The general rule was fixed by Vatican II. It is based on not one, but two principles. This is the actual text:

> The *communicatio in sacris* may not be regarded as a means to be used indiscriminately for the restoration of unity among Christians. Such worship depends chiefly on two principles: it should signify the unity of the Church; it should provide a sharing of the means of grace. The fact that it should signify unity generally rules out common worship. Yet the gaining of needed grace sometimes commends it. The practical course to be adopted, after due regard has been given to all the circumstances of time, place, and persons, is left to the prudent decision of the local episcopal authority, unless the Bishops' Conference according to its own statutes, or the Holy See, has determined otherwise.[22]

The same decree points out, a little further on, that a distinction should be made between the Eastern and Western Churches. Within the Eastern Churches, which have preserved the apostolic succession in the sense understood by the Catholic Church, intercommunion is possible and even advisable in certain cases, but this does not mean to say that it is likely, given the reluctance on the Orthodox side. However, within the Churches and separated communities of the West, there is the issue of an absence of the sacrament of orders as understood by both Catholic and Orthodox. In 1967, the Roman Directory for the application of the *Decree on ecumenism* firmly drew attention to this point.

THE IMPATIENCE OF THE YOUNG

We are troubled and disappointed by an ecumenism which is becoming too institutional and losing its character of a dynamic progress towards the unity which we feel is close at hand. We are ready to accept the slowness and weakness with the courageous advances of our Churches, but we expect those in authority to give real support to the initiatives young people are making in the direction of visible unity. Bound together as we already are in a real communion, sharing a common prayer, we suffer from not being able to share the bread of the Eucharist. We believe that this is in fact depriving us of a privileged means of restoring visible unity. And we hope that the authorities and theologians of our Churches will reconsider this question and will be able to give us a positive answer.

Appeal by the young people gathered at Taizé in 1966.

How hard it is to be patient! Things were easy enough to regulate during the centuries when the Churches ignored each other, hurled anathemas to and fro and had no desire to share each other's Eucharist. However, we are now living in a time when, not everywhere, but in most places, the situation is the reverse. The Churches are rediscovering one another; they respect each other and are beginning to want to share each other's Eucharist. So the bishops have had to exercise great prudence as they tread the knife-edge between loyalty to the rulings of the universal catholic Church on the one hand, and, on the other, the pressing pastoral demands of their own dioceses, especially in the case of mixed marriages.

Different dioceses have behaved differently in specific situations with diametrically opposed results. Sometimes, rigorist measures have resulted; but at other times, there has been a somewhat excessive relaxation of the rules. On the whole, let us say that the bishops have gradually been able to apply the rulings of the Council in a balanced and open manner.

In 1975, a memorandum from the Bishops' Committee for Christian Unity on the eucharistic document produced by the Dombes Group bore strong witness to this attitude:

> The Committee knows and respects the prudent directives of the Holy See in this matter. It also knows of the suffering of certain Christians, especially those in mixed marriages who are generously committed to the unity movement and seek together to deepen their faith but are still separated at that supreme moment of Christian life which is eucharistic communion.
>
> That is why we would like above all to avoid an "all or nothing" position which is theologically dubious and pastorally damaging. So the Committee repeats that it is the responsibility of the bishop to decide on each case which comes before him, taking into account the teachings of the faith, the official directives and the concrete situation of the persons or groups of people involved.

We ask Christians desirous of sharing the Eucharist to think carefully about the meaning and reasons behind their request.

Finally, the Committee hopes that this problem will no longer be seen as a negative sign of contradiction but rather as an opportunity to construct, in faith, a new way of living in the Church, despite the inevitable hardships and tensions caused by our divisions.[23]

This mingling of tradition and innovation was to manifest itself in many ways in the lives of the Churches. As early as 1972, the Bishop of Strasbourg, whose diocese has many Lutherans, with frequent mixed marriages, had decided that new measures could be applied to these cases. He specified certain conditions, under which each partner would be permitted to share in holy communion in the other's Church. In other dioceses, similar rulings were made in specific cases. Inevitably, more people wished to benefit from this dispensation and unfortunately, in certain cases, the rules were somewhat distorted in order to bring Catholic practice more into line with that of the Protestants. This was all the less acceptable because there was also a move in certain circles of the Reformed Church towards a depreciation of ordination. The very word 'ordination' was to be abandoned by the National Synod of Dourdan in 1985, in favour of the new phrase "recognition of ministries", which remained ambiguous (some opting for the same reality under a different name and some contending that the change of name denoted a theological statement).

To clarify things, the Bishops' Commission for Unity published a memorandum on eucharistic hospitality with Christians of the Reformed Churches in France, in 1983. Complicated in content, this memorandum may be summed up by the simple statements made in its two sub-titles: eucharistic hospitality cannot be habitual (for reasons specified); and in certain exceptional cases, eucharistic hospitality may be envisaged (the conditions are given). At first, many Protestants and certain Catholics who were friendly with them, disapproved of the memorandum, because of the opening section. However, a less emotional reading produced a more positive reaction, on account of the second section.

So what exactly are the possibilities of shared eucharistic worship which apply primarily to mixed marriages and "certain ecumenical groups of long standing"? When it is a question of welcoming a Protestant to share the Catholic Eucharist, it is at the discretion of the bishop or his representative, who should discern the motive and the quality of faith; this is exactly as laid down by the Council.

Concerning permission for a Catholic to participate in the Lord's Supper, the memorandum refers to the restrictive measures and rulings of the Roman Directory of 1967 which apply to the universal Church. However, and this is new, in certain exceptional cases, the individual conscience of the Catholic may be taken into account. In order to do this, direct reference is made to the document published by the Synod of the Church in Germany in 1976 which declares that "it is quite possible that Catholics, following their own conscience, may find themselves in a particular situation where participation in the Lord's Supper seems to be a spiritual necessity." However, should they make such a decision, they are reminded that it is contrary to the general ruling of the Church and that they should take care not to endanger their own faith or to scandalize their brothers and sisters.

Thus, in spite of the inevitable discomfort of a divided situation, while maintaining the difficult but necessary loyalty to the rulings involved, the memorandum strove, to take up the phrase already quoted, "to construct, in faith, a new way of living in the Church". So long as a real *metanoia* has not allowed the separated Churches to achieve a better ecclesiastical communion, eucharistic communion, which will be the sign of restored unity, will not normally be able to be shared. The present partial reconciliation already corresponds to a new openness which is a sign of great hope and summons us to even further progress.

As we have already mentioned, the Catholic Church declined the invitation to take part in the founding of the World Council of Churches in 1948, and kept its distance. Yet, even from the Catholic Church's point of view, there were no insurmountable dogmatic difficulties preventing its participation, just as there were none, after the Toronto clarifications in 1950, for the Orthodox Church, whose demands in this matter are broadly the same as those of the Catholic Church.

It can even be said that joining was seriously considered following the Uppsala Assembly in 1968. At Uppsala, where the Pope sent a message which was vigorously applauded, and where 15 Catholic observers were present, two of the main lectures were given by Catholics, one of whom, Fr Tucci, delivered a sensational speech. He started by reassuring those who feared that the Catholic Church "because of its cohesion and numerical importance, might be tempted to take the lead of the ecumenical movement to profit from it according to its own trends." He asserted that, on the contrary, it had no intention of imposing its own ecclesiology and accepted that the dialogue should take place on an equal basis (*par cum pari*) between Churches which worship the same Lord.

He recalled that relationships were developing between the Catholic Church and the WCC, and clearly asked the question, "Must we stop here, at least at this precise moment? Or must we also, from now on, seriously consider the possibility that the Roman Catholic Church could one day become a member of the World Council?" The Assembly's answer was that, if the Catholic Church was to ask for its admission, it would not encounter any obstacle. In a press conference, Fr Tucci went even further, underlining the danger for the Catholic Church of developing its own ecumenical research without using the excellent instrument of the WCC.[24]

Over the following years, during which collaboration

intensified, hope increased again when, at the following Assembly of the WCC in Nairobi in 1975, an Orthodox speaker, Fr Cyrille Argenti, voiced the desire for the participation of all the Churches, "and in particular of the very ancient and venerable Church of Rome, our elder sister..." Following this intervention, a unanimous vote proclaimed, "The Assembly looks forward to the day when the Roman Catholic Church will become a full member of the World Council." The head of the Catholic observers' delegation spoke then to say how touched he was by this unanimous vote.[25]

Already Paul VI, visiting the WCC in Geneva, felt he had to point out that the question was not yet mature and that one needed to reflect on the theological and pastoral implications. At the following Vancouver Assembly of 1983, a message from Cardinal Willebrands implied strongly that things were not going to change immediately, while stressing that ever stronger relationships were building between the Catholic Church and the Council. It is not a question of simple collaboration any more but of *fraternal solidarity*.[26]

Apart form multiple contacts, like the presence of Catholic experts in various sections of the Council, three major achievements deserve special mention:

— The first was the creation of a "Joint Work Group" decided upon as early as 1965 at the central meeting held in Enugu, with the wide aim of "finding some principles which will guide the collaboration and establish the methods to be used." Comprising 12 members of each group, the Joint Work Group still carries on with its patient work.

— Another was in the following year 1966: the permanent collaboration between "Faith and Constitution" and the Roman Secretariat for the preparation of the Week of Prayer for Unity in January, following the line of contacts which had already been established on the initiative of the Christian Unity Centre of Lyon. Each year, 12 representatives, half belonging to the World Council and half to the Catholic Church, meet for a week to establish, with a content acceptable to all Churches concerned, the theme and terms that will be submitted the following year to all the Churches in the world.

– Finally, in 1968, a theological collaboration, already mentioned with the *BEM* and with "Faith and Constitution", was established. Henceforth, 12 theologians selected by the Roman Secretariat were automatically present, one of them, Fr Tillard, even became vice-president of the commission.

Several other attempts at collaboration have strengthened the bonds. There is a Catholic presence in several bodies of the WCC, such as the committee of the Ecumenical Institute of Bossey near Geneva, and the commission Mission and Evangelization which has seven Catholic consultants. There are also contacts with similar organizations in Geneva and Rome, such as the secretariat for help, emergency and reconstruction of CESEAR (Church of help and service committee and assistance for refugees); and Caritas International. Also, there is ongoing communication between the dialogue body of the Council and Pontifical Council for Inter-Religious Dialogue, and the Council's Education and Revival Unit and the International Catholic Bureau for Children.

The creation in 1968 of the Commission for Society, Development and Peace (Sodepax) which did not last, was the only fly in the ointment. Its work quickly became difficult, largely because of the different nature of the mandatory authorities: a Church on one side, and a 'Council' on the other. We saw that the same problem arose with the Seoul Assembly. In 1980, Sodepax gave way to a more modest organization, the "Mixed Social Thought and Action Advisory Group" which itself ceased to exist in 1988.

In all this, we find the continual and complex game of patience and impatience, with justification for both attitudes. Without doubt, the Catholic Church's membership of the WCC would be a sort of cataclysm since the present rules of proportionality would give it the majority of seats on the Central Committee, which would clearly be unthinkable! The rules would have to be amended – a complicated hypothesis, but one to which the Joint Work Group has given some thought. One could, for example, balance the present representation which favours the local Reformed Churches to the detriment of the large Oriental Churches, so that all the 'Church's families', Anglican, Orthodox, Protestant and Catholic, are more equally represented.

The solution may be tied to a deeper problem often unspoken, that of the particular role of the Bishop of Rome in a service for the communion between the Churches. The Catholic Church regards it as inalienable. The other Churches see it as a threat of absorption, because the way this 'service' is usually presented and has been lived through historically during the second millennium is unacceptable to them. One must realize there is more at stake here than the confrontation over the leadership, and that to define the problem in those terms makes it passionate and insoluble!

NOTES

1. Cardinal Willebrands, "Le mouvement oecuménique aujourd'hui", in *DC*, 3 July 1988, p. 664.
2. Faith and Constitution, *Baptism, Eucharist and Ministry*, Centurion and Taizé 1982.
3. *Ministry*, no. 8.
4. Yves Congar, *Chrétiens en dialogue*, p. 25.
5. *DC*, 6 December 1970.
6. *DC*, 3 May 1981.
7. *DC*, 6 May 1973.
8. *DC*, 4 December 1983.
9. *DC*, 18 December 1983.
10. *DC*, 15 January 1984, p. 131.
11. P. Valladier and J.F. Collange, "La Morale dans le dialogue catholique-protestant: terrain d'entente ou de division?", in *Études*, February 1984.
12. *DC*, 3 December 1989.
13. ACAT, *Chrétiens contre la torture*, Édition Cana, 1979, p. 15.
14. Ibid., p. 44.
15. A special issue of *UDC* has been devoted to each of these sessions. The latest of these are: "Prière et unité" (*UDC*, July 1980), "Exigences et urgence du projet oecuménique" (July 1983), "Nos différences

ecclésiales, leur enjeu dans la recherche de l'unité" (July 1986), "Confesser ensemble la foi au Dieu Père tout-puissant, crateur du ciel et de la terre" (July 1989).

16. *DC*, 20 July 1975.
17. Report in *DC*, 6 May 1990.
18. Lukas Vischer, president of the theological department of the Reformed World Alliance, wrote, "The Roman Catholic Church and the World Council of Churches are not comparable organisms. On the one hand, we have a Church, on the other, a community of Churches. That is why they could not have joined together without difficulty. The Vatican leaders saw this very clearly. That is why it is unfair to reproach them for their lack of ecumenical commitment" (in *BSS*, 27 January 1988, p. 4).
19. The "New regulations for mixed marriages" approved by the plenary session of the French Bishops' Conference in October 1970, states: "We know that the promise required of the Catholic partner 'to do all within his or her power to ensure that the children are baptized and brought up in the Catholic Church' has to be fulfilled within the actual circumstances of our home. This means that, having discussed the matter seriously, with due respect for the religious convictions of both of us, we should make a joint decision in accordance with our conscience" (*DC*, 20 December 1970, p. 1131).
The Bishops' Conference has also published a Directory concerning the commitment and vocation of mixed marriages (*DC*, 16 March 1980).
20. René Beaupére, "Les foyers-mixtes dans la vie de l'Église: pastorale et ecclésiologie", *UDC*, April 1982, p. 25.
21. Cf our report: "Les problémes d'‘intercommunion' aujourd'hui. Une réflexion catholique la lumière de l'histoire rècente", *Esprit et Vie*, 27 August-3 September; 10 September-17 September 1987.
22. *Decree on ecumenism*, no. 8.
23. *DC*, 2 February 1975, p. 129.
24. *DC*, 1 September 1968, col. 1479, 1480, 1486, 1489.
25. *DC*, 15 February 1976, pp. 175-176.
26. *DC*, 15 January 1984, p. 103.

Chapter 4

The Christian Churches

AS we have noted, heresies arose from the time of the primitive Church, calling forth condemnations and causing dissidence, yet dying down quickly. Arianism, which denied the divinity of Christ and was condemned at the Council of Nicea in 325, was the only one to last any length of time, especially among the 'barbarian' Germanic peoples, but even it disappeared completely in the sixth century, when Visigoth, King of Spain, converted to Christianity.

Later, three great schisms created the separate Churches which have continued to exist until the present day.[1]

In the fifth century, there was the schism of the ancient Eastern Churches, which separated after the Council of Ephesus (431). This was followed by the formation of the so-called 'Nestorian' Churches, and by the Council of Chalcedon (451), which in its turn was followed by the formation of the so-called 'Monophysite' Churches (Armenian, Coptic, Ethiopian and Syrian). These Churches taken together number about 30 million faithful today.

In the eleventh century, there was the great schism between West and East. The Eastern Church, which had remained faithful to the true faith and was therefore 'Orthodox', in comparison with its neighbours, was from then on known as the Orthodox Church. It has some 170 million faithful today.

Finally, in the sixteenth century, the Reformation shook the West. Western missionary expansion carried this division to other continents in the form of three great Churches: the Catholic Church (some 900 million), the Protestant Churches, themselves divided into various fragmentations (some 380 million), and the Anglican Church (some 70 million). These Churches became somewhat hardened to each other over the centuries of separation, but now they are trying to take a fresh look at each other. They are also seeking to learn from one another spiritually.

A good example of this benevolent, yet at the same time critical look at all the Churches, including his own, may be found in a fine passage from Olivier Clément's dialogues with Patriarch Athenagoras:

> If one considers the three historic branches of Christianity – Orthodoxy, Catholicism and Protestantism – one can discover a complex dialectic between them in which each, from a certain point of view, plays an axial role. The whole experience of my faith leads me to believe that the axis of ultimate integration is the Orthodox Church, because it is the spiritual axis. Orthodoxy shares with Rome the sense of the mystery of the Church; but like the Protestants, the Orthodox demand a certain freedom in the Holy Spirit; however, they do not set prophecy over against sacramental institutions but rather place prophecy within those institutions in order to purify them: for the Spirit rests on the Body of Christ.
>
> Let us now look at the Reformed Churches: they constitute, in a sense, the prophetic axis of the Church. The Reformers did not wish to break up the Western Church. They wished to reform it. Repulsed – and how could it have been otherwise in the absence of the 'Orthodox' spiritual axis? – they opened a chapter of history which will not be closed until Rome, rediscovering its 'Eastern' roots, is able to do justice to their demands without destroying the mystery of the Church. Meanwhile, for Rome, and also for the Orthodox Church, they act as a prophetic goad which prevents both ritual and thought from getting fixed and rigid.
>
> As for Rome, it is the axis of historic incarnation of the universal Church. Only the Catholic Church can prevent Protestantism from melting into history and

Orthodoxy from becoming petrified outside history. But Rome needs the 'Orthodox' spiritual axis in order to respond to the demands of the Reformation without itself becoming Protestant in the narrow sense of that word. And Orthodoxy needs Rome in order to become thoroughly incarnated.[2]

Which Church, looking at the others from its own perspective, could not write lines similar to these, pointing out the profound message of each and inviting it to respond to the questioning of the others? Let us now look at each of these Churches, as they were in former years and as they are now, and let us try to discover the 'spirit' of each.

1. The Orthodox Church

The Orthodox Church – sometimes called Byzantine or Greek, because of its origins – has the typical spirit of the East and embraces other ancient Eastern Churches. To understand this Church's various divisions, we must recall the organization of the ancient Church which was set up around the episcopal sees established in the great cities of the Roman Empire which were reputed to have been evangelized by an Apostle. The head of each of these sees received the title of 'patriarch', which recalled the name attributed to the great ancestors of the tribes of Israel in the Old Testament.

In 325 AD, the Council of Nicea created three patriarchates: Rome in the West; Alexandria and Antioch in the East. A little later, Byzantium became the capital of the Eastern Empire under the name of Constantinople, this city became a fourth patriarchate, to which Jerusalem was added, and the five sees formed the 'Pentarchy', with a well-established order of importance: Rome, Constantinople, Alexandria, Antioch, Jerusalem (Council of Constantinople, 381). The patriarchate of Constantinople had primacy over the whole of the East, Rome over the whole of the West, as well as an honorary primacy over the whole of the Christian world.

The 'genius' of Orthodoxy

The basic value of Orthodoxy, its 'axial' role as Olivier
Clément puts it, is spirituality. This is rooted in the eucharistic liturgy which is at the very heart of the life of the
Church. It is a liturgy which is like a 'sung Bible', abound-
ing with symbols which help us to enter the 'mystery'. It is
a liturgy which seeks to express the beauty of the heavenly
world, which intercedes for the whole world. St Maximus
the Confessor used to say that wherever you celebrate the
liturgy, there is the heart of the world.

One can only urge the Catholic or Protestant who has
not already had this experience, to take part in the Orthodox eucharistic liturgy (reminding them, however, that they
will not be invited to receive communion). Even if they are
disconcerted by a world which seems strange to them (the
length of the celebration, for one thing), they can hardly
fail to feel that they are in the presence of an impressive
ecclesiastical reality. At the moment of the 'grand en-
trance', while the celebrant incenses the sanctuary, the
icons and the people, and the hymn of the Cherubim sounds
forth ("Let us who mystically represent the Cherubim and

sing to the life-giving Trinity the thrice-holy hymn, leave behind the cares of this world . . ."), how can we not feel that the liturgy is a foretaste of heaven, the theme of which is taken up again in the post-communion chant, "We have seen the true light . . ."?

While on the subject of spirituality, we should mention the practice of the Jesus Prayer. The prayer comes straight from the Gospel (Matthew 9:27; Luke 18:12) and is an uninterrupted repetition of the invocation "Lord Jesus, Son of God, have mercy on me, a sinner!" It transfigures life by steeping it in the presence of Christ.[3] The monasteries are the place where this liturgical life is lived to the full, but baptism also calls all Christians to an 'interiorized monasticism' which should impregnate their whole lives.

The presence of holy icons in churches as well as in houses, so characteristic of the East, should also be noted. We often readily welcome them into our Western culture without always knowing and respecting their sacred character. They are seen in the East as "windows opening onto heaven". The cult of the holy icons was not finally accepted until the ninth century, at the end of the long "iconoclastic controversy" between those who took literally the Old Testament commandment: "You shall not make any graven image" (Exodus 20:4) and those who held that after the Incarnation of God in Jesus Christ, the Gospel authorized the veneration of images ("Philip, whoever sees me, sees the Father"; John 14:9). In the end, the second party won and icons came to be widely used in worship.[4]

Certain Christian values receive particular emphasis in Orthodoxy: such as the sense of the presence of the Holy Spirit, which can be seen throughout the liturgy. To receive the Holy Spirit, according to St Seraphim of Sarov, is the aim of the Christian life. Or again, there is the sense of tradition, seen as the wealth of experience of Christians down the ages, beyond the fads and fashions of any particular age. There are several features which contrast with what the Orthodox consider our Western 'legalism'. There is the concept of the unity of the Church for which the

Russians have created the untranslatable word *sobornost* (whose approximate meaning is "conciliation in love"). Or again, in the area of morality, there is the recourse to the principle of 'economy' which, in a particular case where it seems necessary, allows an exceptional relaxation of the rules, in the name of God's loving-kindness. The best known example of this is the possibility of remarriage (with a slightly curtailed ritual) of a spouse who has been the innocent party in a separation.

Of course, every value has its disadvantages, and Orthodoxy does not always avoid these. The liturgy can become a means of escape from the world, and the love of tradition can lead to an unwillingness to make changes in response to the ever-changing questions of humanity. Conciliation in love does not always prevent rivalry between the independent communities which are set up as 'national' Churches, which makes it difficult for the Church to act at a universal level, as can be seen in the slowness of the preparations for the "great and sacred Orthodox Council", still in the preliminary stages. Yet, there are values Westerners could profitably borrow from our Orthodox brothers and sisters. The Eastern awareness of eschatology and the sense of anticipating the heavenly life here below, for example; or the concept of the transfiguration of the world by the living Gospel.

Why the schism?

No doubt these cultural differences were partly responsible for the schism between East and West, but there were many other factors involved. It has been calculated that in the 506 years between Constantine's death (337 AD) and "the Triumph of Orthodoxy" (843 AD), at the end of the iconoclastic controversy, there have been 217 years of separation between Rome and Constantinople. There were seven schisms, before the definitive break of 1054, which itself was not absolute in all places.[5] Let us look just at the main factors involved in this process.

Political factors. The coronation of Charlemagne as Roman emperor by the Pope was considered a sacrilege by the Byzantines who were convinced that only their emperors were successors of the line of Constantine. The fourth Crusade of 1240 was a scandal. The Franks, who had set out to win back the tomb of Christ at Jerusalem, stopped at Constantinople to create a 'Latin Empire', amidst violence and pillage. Pope Innocent III condemned such action when the news reached him, unfortunately too late.

Theological factors. The development in the West of so-called scholastic theology as expounded by such scholars as St Thomas Aquinas is foreign to the Eastern mind. It prefers to adhere to the theology of the Fathers of the early Church, which it considers peerless. The argument over the *Filioque*, in which the Westerners – under pressure from Charlemagne and against the will of Rome which held out against it for two centuries! – added a word to the text of the Latin Creed. The addition stated that the Holy Spirit proceeded not only from the Father, as in the formula of the Council of Constantinople (381 AD), but from the Father "and from the Son". *Filioque* could be justified in terms of Western theological thought, but was unacceptable to the East and constituted a late addition to the text of the Creed (which could not be changed except by another ecumenical Council). Finally and perhaps most significantly, the reinforcement in Rome of a more and more centralized papal authority was unacceptable to the East who saw unity in more 'conciliar' terms. On the one hand, there is the strict and efficient legalism of Rome; and on the other, a collegiate communion, less dynamic and orderly, but seeking to operate in a spirit of greater charity.

For the first millennium, East and West continued in communion despite these difficulties. However, this communion came to an end in 1054 when the fiery Cardinal Humbert visited Constantinople and met with Patriarch Michael Cerularius, who was hostile to the Latins. After an exchange of recriminations, some of which were justified, they ended in a reciprocal excommunication which was to last nine centuries and would lead Constantinople to think of itself as the 'new Rome'. This excommunication was lifted on both sides in 1965 in an ecumenical gesture by Pope Paul VI and Patriarch Athenagoras of Constantinople. However, this did not solve all the problems.

During the centuries, two attempts at re-union were made, the first at the Council of Lyon in 1274; the second at the Council of Florence in 1439. However, they did not last and the capture of Constantinople by the Turks, in 1453, put an end to these attempts at unity.

Failing to achieve unity as a whole, the West tried re-attaching certain portions of the Eastern Church amid pressures from the Catholic States of the West.[6] This 'solution' was understandable as it was based on the then popular notion of a 'return'. In 1596, when a vast region of Polish-Lithuanian territory stretched from the Baltic to the Black Sea, the union of Brest-Litovsk was served by some enterprising Latin clergy. Several Orthodox episcopates of White Russia and West Ukraine signed the union with the See of Rome, on the understanding that the Uniates, as they were to be called, would keep their Eastern rites and customs (the importance of synods, the possibility of ordaining married men, etc.). Then, in 1698, after the victory over the Turks of the House of Hapsburg-Austria, the union of Alba-Julia (Transylvania) saw the beginning of another 'uniate' Church which came under the influence of Western culture and was to support the movement for Romanian independence.

These two 'uniate' communities remained firmly attached to Rome. However, in 1946 and 1948, they were brutally detached by the Communists, one after the other, and were re-attached to the Orthodox Church. The new freedom brought by *perestroika* in the former USSR is now allowing the Christians of these Churches, after years of persecution and clandestine worship, to reclaim their freedom of choice, although not without many obstacles.

There were also other re-attachments to Rome, the most important of which was that of the Melkite Greeks. This term was used for the Syrian Church whose members remained faithful to the faith of Chalcedon after the Syrian Monophysite schism ('Melkites' means partisans of the emperor or king; *malik* in Arabic). A series of attachments, discreet at first and later made public, led to complete union in the eighteenth century, with the Melkite Catholic patriarch having jurisdiction over Jerusalem and Egypt, with the title of "Patriarch of Antioch and all the Orient". There were further re-attachments involving fewer numbers: in Serbia (seventeenth century), in Bulgaria (nineteenth century) and in Greece (twentieth century).

The life of uniate Churches is often difficult in the midst of large Orthodox communities. These unions made before the era of ecumenism are in line with neither the contemporary way of thinking nor with conciliar theology. However, these situations exist and are a product of history, and differ greatly according to the countries concerned. All the partner Churches need to make a courageous effort to find solutions in each case which will be satisfactory to all, and inspired by the spirit of the Gospel. We shall return to this problem later, when speaking of the Catholic Church.

The organization of Orthodox Churches

At present, the Orthodox Church is made up of 15 'autocephalous' ("having their own head") Churches under the primacy of the Patriarch of Constantinople. Each is self-governing, with the right to elect its primate and to consecrate the holy Chrism. These Churches are still faithful to the apostolic canons of the fourth century which state that "A bishop should do nothing – outside what is necessary for his diocese – without the advice of his primate, who should not himself act without consulting all the bishops of his province. Thus concord will reign and God, Father, Son and Holy Spirit, will be glorified by the Lord in the Holy Spirit." These autocephalous Churches fall into several categories:[7]

First, there are the four ancient patriarchates of the East, which now only have a small number of faithful.

1. The ecumenical patriarchate of Constantinople (see at Istanbul), "the first among equals", has barely 20,000 faithful in Turkey itself. To this should be added those of the Greek islands (450,000 faithful), the monastery of Mount Athos, the Greek dioceses abroad and certain other dioceses, which represent several million faithful. Elsewhere, following an ancient ruling of the Council of Chalcedon, isolated Orthodox communities in a foreign country are in theory attached to Constantinople and not to their country of origin. However, the opposite 'racist' attitude is prevalent.

2. The patriarchate of Alexandria has about 10,000 faithful in Egypt and 60,000 to 70,000 in various other countries.

3. The patriarchate of Antioch (see at Damascus) has 800,000 faithful, of whom, 500,000 are in the Middle East.

4. The patriarchate of Jerusalem has 60,000 faithful, including the independent episcopate of Mount Sinai.

Other patriarchates have been established in Europe during the centuries as the Orthodox Church has spread, always requiring the consent of Constantinople (and often granted only after oft repeated requests). These are:

– Moscow, a patriarchate since 1589 (some 50 million practising members and more than 100 million baptized);

– Romania, patriarchate at Bucharest since 1925 (14 million faithful);

– Serbia, a patriarchate since 1920 (9 million faithful);

– Bulgaria, a patriarchate since 1961 (6 million faithful);

– Georgia (1 million baptized). We may note that Constantinople's authorization of this patriarchate, ratifying the existing situation, was not officially 'granted' until January 1990.

In addition, there are six autocephalous Churches which are not patriarchates:

1. Greece (8 million faithful);
2. Cyprus (500,000 faithful);
3. Poland (400,000 faithful);
4. Former Czechoslovakia (150,000 faithful);
5. North America, with the foundation in 1970 of an autocephalous Church which at present comprises 500 parishes. This Church, only authorized by the patriarchate of Moscow, currently represents a part of the Orthodox of the United States, many of whom are still attached to their country of origin;
6. Albania, recognized in 1936 (250,000 faithful, in 1967 – no further reports since then).

Three other Churches have been declared 'autonomous':
– the Monastery of St Catherine of Sinai;
– Finland (60,000 faithful);
– China (60,000 faithful in 1962).

Finally, there are, throughout the world, the 'Churches of the dispersion', which continue to be attached to their Church of origin, in North America (5 million faithful), in South America (600,000), in Europe (700,000) and in Oceania (250,000).

What still separates us?

What separates the East from the West, as we have already said, is above all a different spirit. As Fr Congar wittily expressed it, "between the East and the Catholic West, everything is the same and everything is different, even if it's basically the same thing".[8] As to what separates Orthodox and Catholic on the dogmatic level, the answer varies according to which Orthodox representative you are speaking.

On the one hand, there are theologians and churchmen, of whom the Patriarch Athenagoras was the best example, who think that nothing really separates us. As Pre Scrima, the envoy of the same Patriarch to the Second Vatican

Council, used to say, "Between you and me, we don't need to build up unity, we just need to put it into practice."[9] Yet, on the other, there is a tendency, stemming from the monks of Mount Athos, still to think in terms of absorption and 'return'. Westerners are seen as heretics to be converted, in spite of the solemn lifting of the anathemas and excommunications which took place simultaneously in Rome and Constantinople in 1965. After all, had not the title "the new Rome" been claimed by Constantinople after the schism of 1054, before Moscow claimed the title of "the third Rome" after the capture of Constantinople by the Turks?

So what can we say? It is a fact that the old dogmatic difficulties, which arose in an atmosphere of polemic, the *Filioque* being a prime example, are on the way to being overcome. However, there remain two interconnected difficulties:

1. Historical memories – as a result of the disastrous crusade of 1204, and the existence of the 'uniate' Churches, the East is still wary of what it calls the spirit of proselytism and domination in the Church of Rome.

2. A theological dimension – the East denounces the Roman centralization of the last few centuries, aggravated by the promulgation of new dogmas, above all those relating to the primacy of Rome, which are considered completely unacceptable.

However, even on this last point, avenues of reconciliation seem to be opening up. Note these two particularly well-placed testimonies.

On the Orthodox side, Patriarch Ignatius IV of Antioch, on a memorable visit to France in 1983, declared in an address in Notre Dame Cathedral that "the communion of saints" already unites East and West, and that we should now recognize the communion that exists between us because of the seven great councils we have in common. In a truly eucharistic Church which lives in the Spirit, he added, "the Church could grant to the primacy of Rome those prerogatives necessary to the service of the brethren and to the maintenance of a common witness in faith."[10]

On the Catholic side, we find a similar position taken by Cardinal Ratzinger, who believes that we should be able to come to an understanding. He thinks, on the one hand, the West should not demand, as a prerequisite to communion, that the East accept Catholic dogmatic definitions; then on the other hand, the Orthodox should not require the West to renounce those definitions.[11]

We should also note the new perspectives on the Roman definitions, which were opened up by some memorable words of Pope Paul VI. It was in 1974, in Lyon, during the celebration of the anniversary of the "Council of Union" of 1274. In his message, read by Cardinal Willebrands in the presence of the official Orthodox guests, Pope Paul VI, after having spoken of the great councils of antiquity, mentioned those which had followed them during the centuries of separation, describing them simply as "general Synods held in the West".[12]

Thus, for several decades now, slow progress has been made along the road to communion between the two Churches which successive Popes in Rome and Patriarchs in Constantinople have designated 'sister-Churches'. It is in this atmosphere that dialogues have been developed:

– in 1967, the beginning of the "Dialogue of charity", started at the time of the meetings in Istanbul and Rome of Athenagoras and Paul VI and given impetus by the visit to Rome of Athenagoras' successor, Dimitrios I, in 1988;

– in 1975, the decision to start a theological dialogue on the occasion of the tenth anniversary of the lifting of the anathemas;

– in 1979, the creation of a joint dialogue committee which was to produce regular documents thereafter:

- in 1982, at Munich: "The mystery of the Church and the Eucharist in the light of the Holy Trinity";
- in 1987, at Bari: "Faith, sacraments and unity";
- in 1988, at Valamo: "The sacrament of orders in the sacramental structures of the Church".[13]

2. The ancient Churches of the East

Like the Orthodox Churches, these ancient Oriental Churches separated themselves from the main body of the Church in the fifth century, at a time when East and West were in communion with one another. In theory, the schism was the result of dogmatic differences but there were strong non-theological factors too, in the context of general resistance to the political power of Byzantium. One could say that these are primarily Oriental, non-Byzantine Churches. The 'Nestorians' in fact grew up in the Persian empire of Asia and the 'Monophysites' in Armenia (the Armenian Church), in Africa (the Coptic and Ethiopian Churches) and in the Aramaic-speaking areas of the Roman empire (the Syrian Church). Compared with our Western mentality, these Churches have that Oriental 'genius' already mentioned, but with certain original traits, the study of which is beyond the scope of the present work. The Syrian tradition (or more correctly, 'Syriac') of Antioch for example has, more than any other Church, preserved the spirituality of the first Christian community as it was in the early days after the first Easter and Pentecost. They have also kept the original Aramaic language.[14]

The 'Nestorian' Churches

Nestorius, Patriarch of Constantinople, was accused of holding a false doctrine of the Incarnation: that there were two Persons in Christ and Mary did not give birth to the God by whom salvation came to humanity. In 431, the Council of Ephesus condemned him, affirming that the Word of God had in his own Person been born according to the flesh and that Mary was indeed "Mother of God". The Pope approved the Council, 15 recalcitrant bishops were exiled by the emperor and the unity of the Church seemed to be assured. However, half a century later, there was a schism in Mesopotamia where the Churches announced their independence from the ancient ecclesiastical authorities of the empire. They laid down a definition of their faith in a council supported by theologians, one of whom was the teacher of Nestorius. The bishops of the empire declared these new definitions to be irreconcilable with the faith of the Church, and the Church of Persia was considered to be Nestorian.

This Church has grown remarkably over the centuries, successfully evangelizing the East and Far East. In the Middle Ages, it numbered tens of millions of faithful and had more than 200 dioceses in Asia (Central Asia, Tibet, China, Manchuria, India, Java, etc.). However, the Mongol invasions, and then those of Islam, stopped this expansion and the Nestorian Church was driven into the north of Mesopotamia and the mountains of Kurdistan. In the sixteenth century, the powerful Catholic Church exerted an attraction which brought these 'wanderers' back into the fold, with the formation of a Catholic Church of the

Eastern rite which took the name 'Chaldean'. There were similar returns to the Church of Rome in Cyprus in the fourteenth century, in India and also in Mesopotamia in the sixteenth century.

The case of India led to one of the most perplexing and involved situations of all time. It is worth saying a few words about it, just to show how schisms can sometimes arise. When the Portuguese came at the end of the fifteenth century, the Eastern Christian community which had maintained links with the Nestorian Church, accepted re-integration into the Catholic Church in 1599 and became the Syro-Malabar Church. Later, a certain 'Latinization' of this Church led a large group of its adherents to separate themselves from it in 1653. However, part of this group, rather than return to the 'Nestorian' patriarch whom they had left in the previous century, joined itself to the 'Monophysite' patriarch – the opposite 'heresy'! – and became the Syro-Malankara (or Jacobite) Church. However, a significant number of Christians having chosen to remain Nestorians, quite simply declared themselves independent. Later, the main part of this last group came under the influence of English missionaries who imparted to them a strong Anglican flavour. They took the name of the Mar Thoma Church and as such are now difficult to classify as part of the ancient Eastern Churches. The latest development was in 1930 when the Syro-Malankara Church asked to rejoin the Catholic Church and became the Catholic Malankara Church, attracting many members and leading to even further complications in inter-Church relations! The World Council's figures for the Mar Thoma Church in India, insofar as it is also affiliated to the Nestorian Church, shows 500,000 adherents.

The statistics of the faithful vary considerably according to different sources. For the Eastern Syrian Catholic Apostolic Church, which is the most important part of the Nestorian Church, whose *catholicos* or patriarch resides in Baghdad, the yearbook of the World Council of Churches has the figure of 550,000 members. As for the former Nestorians now re-united to the Catholic Church, there are 280,000 Chaldeans in Mesopotamia and 2,800,000 Syro-Malabar Christians in India.

The 'Monophysite' Churches

At the Council of Ephesus, the theologians of Alexandria had denounced the deviations of the Nestorians of Antioch. However, led by the monk Eutyches, they fell into the opposite error, laying such emphasis on the divinity of Christ that they minimized his humanity. The Council of Chalcedon in 451 condemned the new error, called 'Monophysism', and proclaimed definitively that in Christ there was "a single Person and two natures, without confusion or mixture". Subsequently, three Monophysite Churches detached themselves in succession from the main body of the Church.

The Armenian Church

The Armenian Apostolic Church traces its foundation to the apostles Bartholomew and Thaddaeus. There was much rejoicing when Pope Paul VI returned the relics of St Bartholomew to the Patriarch Vazken I, during a visit to Rome in 1970. It is known that Armenia was the first country in the world to proclaim Christianity as its state religion, on the conversion of its king in 301 AD, 12 years before Constantine's *Edict of Milan*.

At the end of the fourth century, the Armenian Church decided to separate from the mother-Church at Caesarea in Cappadocia, to declare itself independent, under the authority of a *catholicos*. It subscribed to the first three ecumenical councils (Nicea, Constantinople and Ephesus), but did not take part in the Council of Chalcedon. For at that time, Armenia was at the height of its conflict with the

Persians, believing that it was fighting to preserve the Christian world from the contamination of the Persian creed of Mazdaism. It was not until later, and then in a language foreign to them, that the Armenians learned of the decisions made at Chalcedon. They refused to submit to those decisions, which caused the rest of Christendom to consider them as Monophysites. In fact, at the Council of Dvin in 505, the Armenians formally rejected the Chalcedonian formula of the 'two natures' of Christ, which seemed to them a dangerous belief. However, it must be said that they also pronounced solemn anathemas against all heretics including Arius, Nestorius, and even Eutyches, who had founded Monophysism!

The Armenian people have had to suffer Moslem invasions throughout their history; and then in 1915 and the following years, there was the terrible genocide, as is well known, yet they kept their faith. Having at one time had up to 30 million faithful, the Armenian Apostolic Church today numbers about 3.5 million, in Armenia and in the diaspora. This Church has four patriarchal sees, in theory under the authority of the *catholicos* or patriarch of Etchmiadzine. The two main sees are those of Etchmiadzine (Armenia) and Sis (Turkish Cilicia), transferred to Antelias (Lebanon). Two others were added, Jerusalem and Constantinople, but these had few faithful. Since the eighteenth century, some Armenian communities, numbering about 105,000 faithful, have joined the Church of Rome.

The Coptic and Ethiopian Churches

Tradition has it that the Gospel was brought to Egypt by St Mark and it is certain that Alexandria, a Greek city, was evangelized very early on. Later, the Church had a patriarch at Alexandria and a fervent monastic life in the Nile Valley and Delta. The Coptic Church of Egypt (from which it takes its name: Egypt… Gypt… Copt) became separated in 537 when strong opposition to the nomination of a

Greek patriarch at Alexandria led to the appointment of a native patriarch who was found to be Monophysite and led his Church into schism.

Ethiopia was first evangelized around 320 by two Syrian laymen, one of whom was an ordained priest and bishop of Alexandria. Subsequently, as the Monophysite patriarch of Alexandria came to have jurisdiction over the Ethiopian Church, this Church was in turn led into Monophysism. Quite recently, in 1959, the Ethiopian Church achieved independence and the Ethiopians are careful to avoid the name 'Coptic' because of the unfortunate Egyptian connotations of this word.

It is estimated that the Coptic Church of Egypt numbers 7 million faithful. Facing opposition from integrationist elements among the Moslem population of the country, this Church is very lively at present with a considerable growth of monasticism in the same places where the Desert Fathers lived during the early centuries. For its part, the Church of Ethiopia numbers some 14 million faithful. The Coptic Catholic Church (200,000 faithful) and the Ethiopian Catholic Church have come into being as a result of reunion with Rome.

The Syrian Church

Following the Council of Chalcedon, the Christians of the patriarchate of Antioch split into two groups: one Greek and the other Aramaic. In the following century, these two groups became completely separate: the first is 'Chalcedonian' and 'Greek', the second is 'non-Chalcedonian' and 'Aramaic'. The latter was remarkably reorganized by James Baradai, the consecrated bishop of Edessa in 542 through the influence of the empress Theodora. Baradai had leanings towards Monophysism, and he made his Church Monophysite and named it 'Jacobite", after himself.

The Syrian or Syriac Church now exists in the Near East

and in India. In the Near East, the Syro-Jacobite Church of Antioch and all the East has fewer than 100,000 faithful (since 1960 its see has been at Damascus). A part of this Church has rejoined Rome (more than 100,000, with its See at Beirut).

In India, where the patriarchate of Antioch, as we saw, has been growing by the addition of former Nestorians (who had at one time joined the Catholic Church after the coming of the Portuguese) who have formed the Jacobite Church of India. But distances sometimes make communication difficult and this has led to a certain autonomy on the part of this Indian group. In 1980, this Church, from one to two million strong, itself split into two more or less equal groups: the Syrian malankara Jacobite Church, still attached to Antioch-Damascus. The Syrian Malankar Orthodox Church, entirely separated from Antioch-Damascus, having as its leader a *catholicos* resident at Kottayam. (The Syro-Malankara group united with Rome numbers over 300,000 faithful and is growing.)

Ongoing dialogues

There is now a promising dialogue between these Churches and their Orthodox and Catholic counterparts. Between the Orthodox Church and the so-called 'Monophysite' Churches – which all belong to the World Council – a dialogue was set up by "Faith and Constitution" in 1964, followed by several unofficial meetings which resulted in the formation of a commission in 1968. At one of its meetings, in 1978, this commission came to the conclusion that "we have gone beyond the state of schism... There is no longer any dogmatic obstacle". After that, official dialogue was initiated between the Orthodox Church and the ancient Eastern Churches. There were two meetings, one at Chambésy, near Geneva, in 1985, the other in Egypt in 1989. The last of these saw both parties agreed in condemning both Nestorianism and Monophysism.[15]

As for the Catholic Church, there was a decisive assessment of the situation in Pius XII's encyclical *Sempiternus Rex* in 1951, for the fifteen-hundredth anniversary of the Council of Chalcedon. In this document, the language of which is now outdated but the general outlook still prevails, the Pope declared strongly that problems of language and ambiguous translations had unfortunately contributed to the various schisms. He added, "For the reasons we have just given, several groups of Christian dissidents in Egypt, Ethiopia, Syria, Armenia and elsewhere, are straying from the right path only in the words in which they explain the doctrine of the Incarnation of the Lord: which one can deduce from their liturgical and theological books." The commentary on the encyclical, *L'Osservatore Romano* affirmed that it was only by "verbal Monophysism" that they strayed from "the true faith in the mystery of Christ, more in equivocal words than in any substantial deviation of thought."[16]

This was 13 years before the conciliar *Decree on ecumenism*. Since then, many meetings have taken place. Some have been unofficial, through the initiative of the Pro Oriente Institute of Vienna (the fifth meeting was held in January 1990). Others have been more official, notably on the occasion of the visits to Rome of the leaders of these Churches:

— in 1973, after the decision to form a dialogue commission, a delegate of the Coptic Pope Schenouda III visited Rome for talks which resulted in the drawing up of a largely common Creed;

— in 1980, the Syrian Orthodox Patriarch Mar Ignatius Yakoub III and in 1984, his successor, Mar Ignatius Zakka. This last visit was the occasion of a common profession of faith and of a decision to share the sacraments (penance, Eucharist, anointing of the sick) in case of need, which represented a significant step forward. The declaration ends with a solemn commitment to "do all within our power to remove the final obstacles which still stand in the way of full communion."[17]

In 1983, the Patriarch of the Syrian Orthodox Church of India, Baselius Thoma Matthews, also visited Rome and John Paul II met him in India in 1986;

– in 1983, the Armenian Catholicos, Karkine Sarkissian, came to Rome.

– in 1984, the Nestorian Patriarch of the Assyrian Church of the Orient, Mar Dinkha IV;

Without wishing to make undue haste or presuming to predict the outcome, it can be said that full communion is now well on the way.

3. The Churches of the Reformation

Everyone agrees that some kind of reform was necessary in the Western Church at the end of the Middle Ages. But, instead of a renewal of the whole Church, the sixteenth century left us with Western Christendom divided between the Protestant Churches of the Reformation and the Catholicism of the Counter Reformation which was to undertake its own laborious "Catholic Reformation".

We have not yet been able to join together in writing this sad page of history and the historians of both parties have for centuries been giving a mutually hostile, partial and often partisan version of the facts. In a now famous sentence, Pope John XXIII remarked to the observers at the Council, "We are not going to have a historical trial, we shall not try to discover who was right and who was wrong: we all share the responsibility."[18] Let us recall the main points of this period of history.

The lessons of history

At the beginning of the sixteenth century, in a Europe torn by the Hundred Years War and a terrible epidemic of the Black Death – these facts are by way of explanation rather than excuse – the evangelical face of the Church was disfigured by grave abuses. Rome itself had come under the influence of the pagan spirit of the Renaissance and was extremely corrupt. The very throne of Peter was disgraced by the scandalous behaviour of Rodrigo Borgia, Pope Alexander VI. Among the ordinary clergy and people, popular religion had become a matter of endless devotional practices grafted onto a somewhat dubious cult of the saints, and the Gospel was hardly preached at all. The custom of indulgences led to all manner of abuses. One important example, which proved to be the breaking-point for Luther, was the incredible preaching of John Tetzel who travelled through Germany collecting money for the construction of the Basilica of St Peter in Rome, assuring the faithful that as soon as the alms dropped into the collection plate, the soul in Purgatory for which the offering was made would be delivered!

Calls for reform came from all sides. The monk, Luther, was one prophetic voice among many and, incidentally, wished only to reform the Church and not to create a new one. Unforeseeable factors led to the immense success of the movement begun by Luther. The invention of the printing press led to the rapid diffusion of his ideas; the rivalry of the German princes added fuel to the flames, and soon there was serious tension with the Roman authorities. The problem was insoluble, presented as it was in the form of impossible choices – the Bible or the Church, the Pope or the Word of God. The result after several years of fruitless dialogue, with neither side really listening to the other, was the condemnation of Luther in 1521.

However, at the Diet of Augsburg in 1530, it seemed for a time that some agreement was still possible and that the Church had expressed a desire for reform. Pope Adrian VI made a courageous statement which is too little known and which was read by the apostolic nuncio at the Diet of Nuremberg in 1523. Having denounced the misdeeds of Luther, the Pope wrote, "You must say that we freely admit that God has permitted this persecution of the Church because of the sins of men and particularly of priests and

MY CONSCIENCE IS CAPTIVE TO THE WORD

Unless I am convinced by the testimony of Scripture and by cogent reasoning – for I do not believe in the infallibility of the Pope or of the councils, since it has been established that they have often been mistaken or contradictory – I am bound by the biblical texts which I have quoted. As long as my conscience is captive to the Word of God, I cannot and do not wish to retract anything, because it is neither right nor wise to act against one's conscience. So help me God! Amen.

Luther at the Diet of Worms, in 1521

prelates... The whole of Holy Scripture teaches us that the sins of the people stem from the faults of the clergy... We know that even in the Holy See, for a number of years, many abominations have been committed: the abuse of holy things, breaking of the commandments, which has led to scandal. We should not be surprised that the sickness should have spread from the head to the members of the body, from the popes to the prelates. You will promise that we shall do our utmost to start by making improvements in the Roman court, from which perhaps all the trouble has come; it will be the source of healing as it has been the source of the illness... But all this will not be the work of a moment, because the trouble is deeply rooted and takes many forms. We shall be able to go only one step at a time... so as not to increase the present confusion by a hurried attempt to reform everything at once."[19]

In these lines we have a clear admission of the evil and its source, as well as an indication of the way that might have succeeded, that is, a reformation which would have destroyed nothing because it would have taken its time. However, it was too late. There comes a moment where no one is able to control the great collective movements of history.

KNOWING HOW TO ENDURE

I know that in the Church which you call papist, there are many things which I do not like. But I can see the same sort of thing in your Church. But the evils one is used to are more easily borne. So I endure this Church until I can see a better one. And the Church is also bound to endure me until I become a better person.

Reply of Erasmus to Luther,
Mark Lienhard, *Martin Luther*, Paris/Geneva 1983, p. 159

The following centuries saw the Churches in confrontation, each hardening its position. On the Protestant side, the Word was given primacy, with less and less regard for the fact that it was within the Church that the Word was received. On the Catholic side, it was repeatedly said that the hierarchy of the Church must be obeyed as the authentic interpreter of the Scriptures. Although, it was rarely added that the hierarchy itself was at the service of the Word, and that it was the whole Church, drawing on the charisms of all the faithful, which should be applying itself to the understanding and practice of the Word.

As the years went by, the various currents of opinion clashed violently. In Germany, the Peace of Augsburg, in 1555, sought a pacific solution with its decision that the people should follow the 'religion' of its ruler (*cujus regio, ejus religio*), and should leave the country if they were not prepared to do so. In France, the schism led to the bloody wars of religion with the Edict of Nantes (1598). The Catholic State sought progressively to erode the special protection granted to Protestants by this edict, until the time it was finally revoked, in 1685, amidst persecution which would leave its mark for many years to come.

> Christians are the freest of people; having mastery of all things, they are subject to no one. Christians are in all things the best of servants; they are subject to all.
>
> Luther, *Christian freedom*

The 'genius' of the Reformation

One could say, in a certain sense, that the particular genius of the Reformation is the sense of liberty: the liberty of the Gospel over against all the accretions which are so readily added to it; the liberty of the Holy Spirit over all the formulations and institutions in which we always risk stifling him; and the liberty of the Church with regard to human authorities.

Protestantism at its best was the end-product of an immense effort to achieve the evangelical reform which the Church needed. This can be heard in the striking formulae of the first days of the Reform: *Sola fides... Sola scriptura... Sola gratia* (faith alone... the Scriptures alone... grace alone). The genius of the Reformation lies in the merciless struggle for evangelical purity, and this is its 'axial' message of a prophetic nature. Christians of other Churches should understand this clearly. In 1983, the five-hundredth anniversary of Luther's birth, Cardinal Etchegaray wrote in the Catholic newsletter of his diocese of Marseilles, "Luther is a Christian straight out of the Gospel. He wanted the Church to fight for its one true cause: to ensure that the Gospel shone through a Church which was weighed down with excess baggage..."[20]

NEGLECT OF THE WORD

Someone will say to me: what crimes, what scandals, this fornication, drunkenness, mad addiction to gambling, all these vices of the clergy!... These are grave scandals, I admit; they should be denounced, they should be remedied; but the vices of which you speak are visible to all; they are grossly material; they are perceptible to one and all; so people are troubled by them... Alas for this evil, this incomparably more harmful and cruel pest: the conspiracy of silence about the Word of truth or its adulteration; this evil is not grossly material, people do not even see it, they do not fear it...

Sermon by Luther, 1512

This is the profound and abiding question that the Reformation addressed to all the Churches and particularly to the Catholic Church. However, the Cardinal goes on to say, in the same letter on Luther, "But, in so doing, he discarded the priceless treasures of the undivided Church and his heirs have not been able to realize the totality of the faith of the Church in its continuity down the centuries." This is the criticism that the Catholic Church, and others, can level at the Churches which grew out of the Reformation.

The Protestant Churches today

Through the centuries, the Reformation spread beyond its first area of expansion – Luther's Germany, the France and Switzerland of Calvin, the Switzerland of Zwingli – and came to the other countries of Europe, then to America and all the other continents. At the present time, some 380 million Protestants share the heritage of the Reformation. After the Lutherans and the Calvinists, the latter preferring to be called Reformed or Presbyterian according to their different countries, there came into being different 'Evangelical' Churches. Some of these have become very large Churches, such as the Baptists and the Methodists, and at the beginning of our own century, in a somewhat separate category, the Pentecostals. Even if these Evangelical communities do not always engage in dialogue, one should be careful not to confuse them with 'sects' – they are authentic Christian Churches.

The Lutheran and Reformed Churches

There are some 67 million Lutherans throughout the world. In Europe, there are 48 million (the majority in Germany and Scandinavia); some 10 million in America (especially in the North); 4 million in Asia and the same number in Africa, where their missions are flourishing. For example, in Ethiopia, the Lutheran Church, 'Mekane Yesu', has grown in a few decades from 20,000 to 500,000 members; and 800,000 in Oceania. Most Lutherans are members of the World Lutheran Federation which was officially formed in 1947, although 13 million of them do not belong to this body, and 3 million are members of the strict Church of Missouri in North America. Their basic doctrinal document is the Augsburg Confession of 1530.

Since it has retained many elements of the undivided Church, including the episcopate which poses problems both of origin and succession, the Lutheran Churches often seem to Catholics to be quite close to their own Church. An extreme case is the Lutheran Church of Sweden which remained almost intact after the schism, with bishops who are convinced that they are part of an unbroken apostolic succession.

The Reformed Churches number some 52 million membership. There are 14 million in Europe, mainly in Switzerland and Scotland, where they are known as Presbyterians. In France, they are the largest Protestant denomination; in Africa, there are 17 million, mainly in South Africa; in North America, 12 million; in Asia, 7 million; and in Oceania, 2 million. Most of these Churches are members of the Reformed World Alliance, founded in 1875. Reformed Protestantism often seems to Catholics to be very different from their own Church. There is a certain austerity in the liturgy and decor of the Churches (a bare cross instead of the Lutheran crucifix, the simple black dress of the pastor or even a total lack of liturgical ornaments); and a greater importance is given to preaching than to the celebration of the Eucharist.

Now, there is a move towards unity between the Lutherans and the Reformed, who practise intercommunion with increasing frequency. In Europe, in 1973, most of the Lutheran and Reformed Churches signed a theological agreement on the essential points of faith and order in the Churches known as the "Concord of Leuenberg". At world level, a joint commission for dialogue between the Lutheran World Federation and the Reformed World Alliance was set up in 1985.

The Evangelical Churches

Let us begin with certain necessary clarifications, because the word 'Evangelical' is used in three different senses. It can be added to the title of one of the Protestant Churches – so one may speak of "The Lutheran Evangelical Church"; it may denote a tendency within a Church – so one can speak of the Evangelical wing of the Reformed Church; and, it may mean a certain number of specific Churches, which may be marked by three particular characteristics:

1. They are above all Churches of the Bible. The Bible is understood as the only guide to faith and conduct, which leads to a strong distrust of ecclesiastical traditions, creeds and confessions of faith. More than any other Protestant, an Evangelical is one who, when faced by any kind of problem, will first ask, "What does the Bible say?"

2. They are Churches of those who profess the faith (sometimes they are called 'confessing' or 'believing' Churches), where the members are only those who have made a personal act of faith, following a conscious conversion. This is why the Evangelicals are opposed to those Churches which they call 'multitudinist' where little heed is paid to the Christian quality of the members, who may have no more than a sociological link with the Church (among which they classify the Lutherans and Reformed as much as the Catholics). As a result, baptism – usually by immersion – is only administered by the Evangelical Churches to the spiritually adult, who are capable of personal commitment. Hence, they do not baptize small children. This 'professing' character naturally leads to a missionary spirit: every Evangelical Christian is a missionary.

3. They are Congregational Churches, in which the 'congregation', that is, the local Church or parish, is responsible for itself, without having any personal or synodal authority of any sort over it. If these Churches sometimes find themselves meeting on a wider basis, it is not in Synods but in congresses, which are simply places to meet, reflect and help one another; such meetings never result in any sort of ruling to be imposed on the Churches.

As a member of one of these Churches put it, Evangelical Churches consist of the Bible and freedom, with all that this last word suggests in the way of complete freedom of conscience. There are no binding dogmas, no baptism of children before a responsible age, all in a context of absolute separation from the State.

Most of these Evangelical Churches are Evangelical Baptist Churches which number some 36 million baptized members, to which we should add the considerable number of non-baptized who participate in the life of the Church while preparing for baptism.[21]

The origins of the Baptists are instructive. Historically they stem from the Anabaptists of Zurich, that branch of extreme Protestantism which sought to rediscover the primitive purity of the Gospel and to live it in complete independence of the civil authority. Rejected and persecuted on all sides, by Protestants as well as by Catholics, these scattered Anabaptists formed isolated, groups, without any leadership. In 1536, Simon Menno, a Catholic priest converted to Anabaptism, set about establishing order in the denomination, and so founded the Mennonite Churches which have survived to this day (600,000 worldwide).

The Baptist Churches date back to these Mennonite Churches by way of English Calvinist dissidents who took refuge in Holland and were attracted by their Evangelical quality, although they were perplexed by their absolute non-violence. Returning to England, some of these English-speaking Dutch founded Baptist Churches properly so called, which later spread to America where they now form the largest Protestant group, including such well–known names as Martin Luther King, Billy Graham; the cosmonaut, Irving; and former President Carter.

Aware of their extreme interpretation of Reformation principles, Baptists like to describe themselves as 'radical' Protestants. Throughout the world, their Churches are of varied aspects, from the large, rather 'established' and multitudinist Churches of the USA to the small, courageous, missionary communities of Russia. Moreover, some belong to the World Council of Churches, while others denounce this body as being anti-evangelical.

The Evangelical umbrella covers many small Evangelical Churches impossible to number and often having only a few adherents. On the fringe may be found the Adventists, who are not generally considered to be a Church, even though this situation seems to be changing at present.

To the Evangelical Churches, we can also add the Methodist Churches, formed in the eighteenth century from a revival movement in the Church of England centred round two Anglican priests, the brothers John and Charles Wesley. Their movement began with a students' association whose spiritual growth the Wesleys strove to nurture by a rule of life (*methodus vitae*) which won them the mocking title of 'Methodists', which they later decided to keep.

A little later, the Wesleys' preaching began to draw crowds and the brothers became leaders of a strong revival movement, but the Anglican Church, finding their enthusiasm excessive, rejected them. After that, a Methodist Church came into being and spread throughout the English-speaking world. There are some 50 million Methodists in the world. They differ from country to country (being close to the Reformed Churches in Europe but 'Episcopal' in America), but their common characteristic is a special emphasis on conversion of hearts through the evangelical preaching of salvation. In 1951, a World Methodist Council was formed.

Pentecostal Churches

Pentecostal movements appeared at the beginning of the twentieth century in Protestant circles in the United States and in Great Britain. They were 'revival' movements starting from a rediscovery of the presence of the Holy Spirit and his action in the lives of believers. Their aim was to rediscover the atmosphere of the primitive Church as it is described in the Acts of the Apostles, with the conviction that the Spirit will manifest himself, today as in former times, with the fullness and power of his charisms, including healing, the gift of tongues, etc.

Soon rejected by many Reformed Churches who were wary of its turbulent character, the movement was organized into communities which have various names: the Assemblies of God, which is the largest, the Evangelical Revival Churches, etc. All of them seek to rediscover the Gospel in its freshness and are attractively dynamic. Like the Evangelical Churches, the Pentecostals practise baptism by immersion, administered to believers only, but they also have the "baptism of the Holy Spirit". This is the presence of the Holy Spirit, generally experienced amid the fervour of a prayer meeting. As a rule, someone who has not received the baptism of the Holy Spirit and the gift of tongues may not exercise authority in the Church.

Like all Evangelical Churches, the Pentecostals are de-centralized and united only by regional, national and world 'conventions'. Baptisms, celebrations of the Lord's Supper, anointing with oil and laying on of hands on the sick are all features of the life of the community. They generally read the Bible in a 'fundamentalist' way, favouring the literal meaning and showing a profound distrust of the 'erudite' interpretations of exegetes and theologians. There are more than 50 million Pentecostals in the world.

We should add that the charismatic renewal, which has recently appeared at the heart of the Catholic Church, also originated in America as a result of contact with the Pente-costal Churches. When it began, a commission of the American episcopate decided that it was just a renewal movement within the Catholic Church and that it should be favourably received, as long as the hierarchy kept a watchful eye on it, which it did. From time to time, the movements of charis-matic renewal in the Catholic Church and the Pentecostal Churches make contact, but the Pentecostals remain wary and critical of the Catholic Church as a centralized institu-tion, disapproving of some of its practices, especially the place it gives to Mary.

What separates us

Are we separated by the theology of 'justification'? Protestants, following Luther, insist on justification by faith and denounce the Catholic theology of human beings, by the grace of God, co-operating in their own salvation. Centuries of controversy, on both sides, have asserted that we are separated by our respective theologies of justifica-tion, and many Christians continue to think so. However, the non-polemical reflection, which has been going on for

109

several decades now, is in the process of ending this conflict, in both theological works and extended dialogue.[22]

Let us approach the matter from a different angle. To explain things in a simple but profound way, let us say that what separates Protestants from Catholics, as well as from the Orthodox, is a debate about fidelity to the will of Christ, which can be summed up by two corresponding accusations:

a. the Protestant accusation, "You have added to the Gospel!"; the accusation of the other Churches, "You have diminished the deposit of faith!" We can find these accusations or their equivalents in all previous areas of conflict, but today there is a real effort to engage in constructive dialogue about authority in the Church, the institution of the papacy, the sacraments, the role of Mary, etc.

b. The Catholic accusation says, "In reaction against abuses which we also deplore, you have decided to base your faith on the Gospel and sweep away everything else, but it seems to us that you have gone too far and lost essential elements of the deposit of revelation. Why not agree to reflect upon what you 'lack' in the matter of the episcopate, the universal ministry of the Church, the Eucharist to which you sometimes attach such little importance, to the place of Mary in the New Testament, etc.?"

The quality of dialogue may be improved by raising it to a theological level. This is the task to which the joint committee of Catholic-Protestant dialogue in France has recently set itself. Both Catholic and Protestant theologians agreed that the basic problem is the role of the Church in salvation. Can it be said that the Church is the "instrument of salvation"? Can it be said that the Church is sanctified to the point of becoming itself sanctifying?

The Catholic answer, based on the sacramental quality of the Church, is in the affirmative. Salvation is, of course, due to the pure grace of God, but the Church 'co-operates' in the work of salvation, being "a steward of the mysteries of God" (cf 1 Corinthians 4:1). It celebrates the sacraments as concrete acts of salvation, effective here and now.

The Protestant answer is that, if the Church is indeed the instrument of salvation which God uses to advance the Kingdom ("the saw with which God cuts down the tree", as Luther said), this Church, in the name of salvation through grace alone, is always a second cause, entirely subordinate to the first cause. The Church "creates in humanity the willingness which allows God alone to accomplish the good."

Having laid this down, and so replaced the sterile confrontations of the past with a readiness to listen to the other side, the joint committee concluded with two related recommendations:

The first recommendation asks each Church to admit that it is prone to a particular and clearly defined temptation. It is for each Church to listen to the warnings of the other to avoid falling into its particular temptation. The specifically Catholic temptation is to "identify the Church with Christ, the body with the Head, forgetting the no less fundamental distinction between the Bride and the Bridegroom." The specifically Protestant temptation is to think that "the visible Church remains an entirely human reality, in some way outside the mystery to which it bears witness."

The second recommendation is an extension of the first and invites us to take a step further. We must quote this profound text which is rich in meaning in its entirety:

What we have to do, on both sides, is to seek to reduce or overcome whatever still remains today as a divisive difference, in order to transform it into a difference that is compatible with unity. This will be done once we have integrated our respective viewpoints in a wider and fuller comprehension of the mystery which has been entrusted to us. We shall each have to pay closer attention to the *irremovable part of the truth* to which our partner bears witness. It will not be enough to arrive at a fundamental consensus which does not affect the actual existing situation. That is why we need not only

111

'conciliation' but 'reconciliation', to be achieved through the conversion of each party.[23]

This is, in fact, what is being tried, with varying degrees of success, in the dialogue of today.

Entering into dialogue

Let us speak first of all of dialogue at the grassroots level. Most of the time, when people meet those whom they already know and the encounter is relaxed and friendly, the atmosphere is excellent. There is an ardent desire for unity and for a common testimony in all areas, especially those of peace, justice and the conservation of the environment. In more formal meetings, there may still be an exemplary level of charity and truth.

It can happen, it must be admitted, that one meets more difficult situations where there is a sense of anti-Catholicism stemming from the historical memory of past troubles; and this feeling is sometimes kept alive by certain sectors of the press. For example, a delegation of the World Council of Churches which went to France in 1984 to meet the French communities, remarked on the "defensive attitude to the past adopted by the Protestants whom we met, some of whom were definitely anti-Catholic".[24] Various books in recent years bear witness to unease among Protestants who feel themselves to be in the minority, and are seeking to rediscover their identity and their message, often with a certain aggressive triumphalism.

To be honest, we must add that plenty of Catholics, too, continue to nurture vague anti-Protestant feelings and are also to be blamed for certain difficult situations where dialogue ends in an impasse because each side sees that the other has a completely different set of rules. Sometimes the ecumenical Catholic seems to be confronted with a Protestant who is still living in the age of credal conflict and who has said farewell to ecumenism. Sometimes, on the contrary, the ecumenical Protestant may seem to be faced by a representative of a Catholic Church which is in a large majority and is secretly threatening, scornful of minority groups, and playing the game by its own rules. We should all examine our consciences on the question of latent tendencies to absorption and resistance to *metanoia*.

At world level, there has been an increase of major dialogues between Churches for the last 20 years. Let us mention only those in which the Catholic Church has taken part. Some of these dialogues are only at the stage of friendly meetings where people get to know one another, but the positive thing is that they continue to happen, even if progress is slow. This is the case with the Methodist World Council (since 1967), the Pentecostals (since 1971) and the Evangelicals (since 1977).

The dialogues begun with the two oldest Protestant groups which grew out of the Reformation, the Lutherans and the Reformed, have been somewhat different in character. The dialogue with the Reformed World Alliance has been laborious. Started in 1970, it experienced an initial phase of limited progress which ended in 1977 with a text entitled "The presence of Christ in the Church and in the world",[25] which was modestly qualified as an "exchange of views". After several years of inactivity, the Commission set to work again in 1984, with a complete change of membership, and pondered the theme of the Church as "People of God, body of Christ, temple of the Holy Spirit".

Progress has been the most spectacular with the Lutherans of the Lutheran World Federation. This dialogue started in 1967 with texts on the Eucharist and then on ministry. Before long, attempts were made to imagine concrete means of re-establishing communion, and the last text, "Facing Unity", considers openly what would be the stages towards the recovery of full communion between the Catholic Church and the Churches belonging to the Lutheran World Federation. In broad terms, it would be a matter of a four-part process:

1. the development of all that is already in existence;

2. then a first official act of mutual recognition (with the possibility of sacramental communion, with the aim of moving to full communion eventually);

3. then there would be the common exercise of a form of episcopate which could be personal or collegiate in which the Churches would be truly united without being absorbed;

– finally, there would be the creation of a common ecclesiastical ordained ministry, with new ministers, broadly adapted to local conditions.[26]

Naturally, these are only proposals made by the Lutheran World Federation on the one side and the Catholic Church on the other and the two bodies are now examining them in detail, but the very existence of such a text is already an important occurrence. Fr Congar describes it as "a quite sensational document" and expresses his astonishment at the serious nature of the work already undertaken, concluding that here "we are in the presence not of dreams but of real possibilities."[27]

4. The Anglican Communion

Sometimes ill-informed people think of Anglicans as a category of Protestantism. This is a misunderstanding of Anglican originality. The circumstances of separation and the history of the last few centuries provide ample proof. When speaking of the breaks in the unity of the West, the conciliar *Decree on ecumenism* includes a special place for Anglicans, "Among [the communities separated from the See of Rome] who preserve in part Catholic tradition and structures, the Anglican Communion has a special place" (no. 13).

After its evangelization, the high point of which was St Augustine of Canterbury and his companions being sent by Pope Gregory I, England had always remained in complete union with the See of Rome, even if its insular position had kept it, in some respects, at a cultural distance from the European continent. In the same year as the condemnation of Luther, in 1521, Pope Leo X rewarded King Henry VIII with the title *Defensor fidei* for his fine defence of the Catholic faith against the Reformer.

A few years later, however, the schism began, with the same King Henry VIII, to whom the Pope refused the annulment of his marriage with Catherine of Aragon so he could marry Anne Boleyn. Henry VIII obtained this annulment from the Archbishop of Canterbury and proclaimed himself head of the Church of England, which earned him excommunication. After, Thomas More, the Chancellor, and John Fisher, the Bishop of Rochester, had been put to death for opposing the king, England settled into a state of schism, without ever actually becoming Protestant.

Hence, the Reformation began to exert its influence on the Church of England very early, where it met adverse reactions on the part of Catholics. First, there was a short and brutal Catholic reaction during the reign of Mary Tudor (1553-1558), daughter of Catherine of Aragon. It was followed by the longer Protestant reaction of Elizabeth I, who became queen in 1558. The two strands continued to co-exist and came to the fore in succession. In the seventeenth century, there was a Puritan movement of Calvinist origin (at the same time that John Knox was founding the Presbyterian Church in Scotland). Then, in the eighteenth century, there was the pietist movement out of which came the Methodist Church. Then, in the nineteenth century, the Oxford Movement, 'Catholic' in inspiration, whose leader, Newman, was to join the Church of Rome.

The 'genius' of Anglicanism, to use the word applied to the other Churches, is the product of this historical heritage, which allows this Church to describe itself as both 'catholic' and 'reformed'. They are right, in a way, because the Anglican Church has at its heart the constant juxtaposition of an 'Anglo-Catholic' wing (the so-called High Church) and an 'Evangelical' wing (the so-called Low Church), and even a third category, 'modernist' in character, called Broad Church. The labels 'Catholic' and 'Protestant' are appropriate because each of these wings is continually influenced by the other. Those familiar with the Anglican Church know there is no Anglo-Catholic who

THE ANGLICAN CHURCH,
A 'BRIDGE-CHURCH'

It is not easy for non-Anglican Christians to understand the difficulty which modern Anglicans find when faced with ecumenical dialogue. During the first stages of dialogue, Anglicans seem to be in a particularly favoured position; their exceptional history, the desire of the Anglican Church to be 'Catholic' and 'Evangelical' at the same time, the 'comprehensiveness' expressed by the co-existence of different theological traditions, all these factors apparently give the Anglican Church the providential vocation of a 'Bridge-Church' between Catholicism and Protestantism. But as one goes on, one sees that the path is a hard one to travel... But we are all the same in a unique position, obliged as we are by our history and our vocation to hold out one hand to the Roman Catholic and Orthodox Churches, the other to the Churches of the Reformation. It is not surprising that we are often torn in two.

Roger Greenacre, Canon of Chichester,
The Four Rivers, no. 20, pp. 71-72

has not received something from the Evangelicals, nor any Evangelical who does not accept, in some form or other, some element of Catholic thought.

Owing to its unique position, the Anglican Church likes to think of itself as a 'Bridge-Church', presenting a picture of what the re-united Church of the future might be. The same unusual flexibility may be found beyond the confines of the Church of England. For example, in the Anglican Communion, which is not to be confused with it, even if the Church of England comprises nearly half of all Anglicans and exercises a sort of leadership over the whole of the Communion. Anglicanism has in fact spread all over the world, starting with the countries once under British influence, and now includes some 30 Churches, some of which do not even speak English, but French, Spanish or Japanese. Each of these member-Churches is independent, with its General Synod led by its bishop-primate. The organic link between them is the Lambeth Conference which takes place every 10 years at the invitation of the Archbishop of Canterbury. The 500 or so bishops of the Communion meet together, and although any resolutions they may make are not binding, they nevertheless have a real moral authority.

Of course, this freedom and 'comprehensiveness' which is an Anglo-Saxon trait, also has its disadvantages, especially the absence of authority and pastoral regulation at the level of the Communion. This was all too clear at the Lambeth Conferences of 1978 and 1988 where those for and against the ordination of women to the priesthood and episcopate met in violent opposition. Having come very near to breaking-point, the Communion was not in fact destroyed, but has certainly been weakened.

The Anglican Church today

So the Anglican Communion is made up of some 30 Churches, with about 70 million faithful, of whom almost half are in England itself, with more than 500 bishops (rather unequally distributed: 44 diocesan bishops in England, 128 in black Africa). From the doctrinal point of view, Anglicanism has no particular confession of faith, but proclaims its adherence to the faith of the undivided Church. Its particular features are:

– the Book of Common Prayer which is at the heart of Church life and is used by both clergy and laity. It contains, as well as all the ritual, a form of liturgical prayers for the morning (Matins) and for the evening (Evensong), to which all are invited. The fourth edition, made in 1662, with the elimination of certain 'Protestant' elements, is still valid, alongside a modern revision made in 1980;

– what is usually called the Lambeth Quadrilateral: the Bible; the ancient confessions of faith (the Nicene and Apostles' creeds); the sacraments, especially baptism and the Eucharist; the historical episcopate. The latter clearly marks the difference between Anglicanism and Protestantism in general.

Without any sort of formal authority over the Communion as a whole, co-ordinating bodies have gradually grown up, being convened by the Archbishop of Canterbury. Since 1878, there is the Lambeth Conference, where all the bishops meet every 10 years. Then, there is the Anglican Consultative Council, which since 1968 has been a permanent body for making contact between the Churches. Then, there is the Committee of Primates, made up of the presiding bishops of each Church, which has convened since 1978.

It is well-known that the Church of England is 'established', that is, linked to the civil power. The sovereign is 'head' of the Church and he or she appoints the bishops who are nominated by the Prime Minister, to whom two names are given by a Church commission. Moreover, Parliament has the right to veto the motions of the Church Synod. However, none of the other Churches of the Communion is 'established', and, as far as the Church of England itself is concerned, these constraints are often mere formalities.

The Church of England has been a member of the World Council of Churches from the beginning and has always shown a keen desire to enter into dialogue. Anglicans have regular meetings with the Orthodox and the ancient Eastern Churches, as well as with the Lutheran Churches. They established inter-communion with the Old Catholics in 1931. In England itself, an attempt at union (The Covenant) between the Anglican Church and four other Churches (the Methodist Church, the United Reformed Church, the Moravian Church and the Churches of Christ) nearly succeeded, but finally failed in 1982.

Schisms start easily enough but seldom end. They produce horrible symptoms: each side forms a false idea of the beliefs of the other and whatever the other side says is taken out of context and interpreted in thought-forms which are foreign to it. The rift widens, becoming self-perpetuating; that is to say that Christians are divided mainly because they are divided and then the schism becomes its own justification.

Twelve years of working with ARCIC have convinced me that the greater part of the disagreements between Canterbury and Rome stem from words rather than facts.

Henry Chadwick,
Christian Unity, April 1984, p. 15

As far as the Catholic Church is concerned, the historical memory of English Catholics was for a long time an obstacle to ecumenism. We must not forget that Catholics were for a long time considered as second-class citizens (in 1689, the Act of Tolerance did not apply to Catholics, who did not enjoy freedom of worship until 1791, and only in

1829 were they granted equal rights). But things have changed considerably and dialogue is now at an advanced stage. We have already mentioned the initiatives of the forerunners (Lord Halifax, Père Portal, Cardinal Mercier). During the last 30 years, there has been an increasing number of top-level meetings: the visits to Rome of the Archbishops of Canterbury (Fisher in 1960, Ramsey in 1966, Coggan in 1977, Runcie in 1989); and the visit to Canterbury of Pope John Paul II in 1982.

Above all, a stable institution for dialogue was set up in 1970 known as ARCIC (Anglican-Roman Catholic International Commission). Between 1971 and 1981, it produced a series of important documents on the Eucharist, ministry and ordination, and authority in the Church, which were published together as a *Final Report* in 1982.[28] The work continues with ARCIC II, the commission established at Canterbury in 1982, which published its findings in *Salvation and the Church* in 1987 and *The Church as communion* in 1991.[29]

What is it that still separates us?

From the point of view of Anglicanism, the difficulty rests on the nature of the authority of the Bishop of Rome, but the ARCIC texts on authority have begun to clear the path. "We believe that the primacy of the Bishop of Rome can be affirmed as part of God's design for universal *koinonia*, within the terms compatible with our two traditions."[30] On the same vein, the Archbishop of Canterbury, at the time of his meeting with John Paul II in Rome in 1989, took up again – not without unlatching reactions within his Church – the question he had put to the last Lambeth Conference: "Must not all Christians reconsider the kind of primacy that the Bishop of Rome has exercised in the primitive Church, a 'presidency in charity', for the good of the unity of the Churches, in the diversity of their mission?"[31] Will this be sufficient for the Catholic Church? We will again meet the question in the last chapter.

The difficulties of the Catholic Church concern ordination. One of them is old; the other, more recent.

Old difficulty: *the validity of ordinations* in the Anglican Church after the separation. Raised in the nineteenth century, as the time of the first approach, the question was examined by a Roman commission which concluded negatively in 1896. A better historical knowledge of the origins and a more ironic climate led the Catholic Church to new approaches. In a letter to the presidents of ARCIC II, Cardinal Willebrands explained the new context in which the question of ordination was situated: the evaluation process initiated by the current dialogue – he wrote in a well studied language – could lead the Catholic Church to establish that the text of ordination could no longer remain the obstacle that had been at the basis of the judgement of Leo XIII in 1896, that it could "lead to a new evaluation by the Catholic Church of the sufficient character of these Anglican rites for all that concerns future ordinations".[32] They pave a new way forward.

Recent difficulty: *the ordination of women* in the Anglican Church. Inaugurated in Hong Kong in 1944 and in 1971, the practice of ordaining women progressively caught on the other Churches of the Anglican Communion under pressure from the feminist lobby and women's rights groups. In 1978, the Lambeth Conference acknowledged the diversity of the practices, but made clear that ordained women could not exercise their ministry in the Churches that did not approve and accept such ordination. In 1988, at the start of the new Lambeth Conference, where the opposing currents vehemently confronted each other to the point that it was considered that the Anglican Communion was "enfeebled", there were 1270 women-priests in the seven Churches of the Anglican Communion (Hong Kong, USA, Canada, New Zealand, Kenya, Uganda, Brazil).[33] In the years that followed, the practice spread to other Churches (Ireland, South Africa, Australia...). The issue of the ordination of women took a critical turn when some women were ordained *bishops* in the USA (1988 and 1990) and in New Zealand (1990).

The Church of England has been hesitant and divided. The supporters of the ordination of women maintain that Scripture does not contradict it in a clear manner. They argue that tradition has sometimes known unforeseen developments, and that theologically there is nothing against a woman "representing" Christ, since the Incarnation has assumed all humanity. Those opposing the ordination of women, besides the profound symbolic argument that holder of a pastoral charge "represents" Christ Head of the Church (in a symbolism where the Church is espoused to Christ), raise an ecclesiological objection: it is very imprudent for a Church to take a decision that contradicts tradition, without a concerted effort and walking together with the other Churches, notably the Catholic and the Orthodox. In 1975, the General Synod of the Church of England, while declaring that it had no fundamental opposition to ordination, concluded that the time was not yet ripe.

Once the seed has been planted such issues always develop and progress. In 1988, the Church of England accepted that women could be ordained deacons. In 1991, Dr Runcie, Archbishop of Canterbury and Primate of England, was replaced by Dr Carey, a firm supporter of the ordination of women. On 11 November 1992, with a very slim majority, the General Synod of the Church of England decided that women could be ordained to all the ministries of the Church.[34] The decision generated a great emotional upheaval and identity crisis in the Church of England, where a number of bishops and priests considered seriously, reflecting on the various possible modalities, of leaving their Church. At the time of writing this, it still awaits ratification, as the 'established' character of the Church of England enjoins that the text be examined and judged 'expedient' by the Parliament before being submitted for the signature of the Sovereign.

Since we cannot foresee the future, the only thing we can say is that the Catholic Church, whilst reaffirming that the new practice does not correspond to its teaching, is very attentive in not aggravating the difficulties of the Anglican Church, and continues to dialogue.

5. The Catholic Church

Our review of the ancient schisms between the Churches has given us the opportunity of seeing the part played by the Catholic Church. Moreover, what we have said of the dialogues and meetings of each Church also concerned the Catholic Church. So without repeating that history, we can limit ourselves here to the message of the Catholic Church itself at the present time.

The 'genius' of the Catholic Church

Having paid due respect to the 'genius' of each of the great Churches and also mentioned their limitations, I now feel free to stress in the same way the 'genius' which is proper to the Catholic Church, as well as the temptations to which it is prone, and which it does not always resist.

Olivier Clément, whom we took as our guide, described the Catholic Church by saying that it represented "the historical axis of Incarnation in the universal Church". In a word, we could say the 'catholicity' of the Church in time and space. Let us try to develop this point.

In a special issue of the review *Christian Unity* devoted to the Catholic Church, whose articles were written "under the eyes of our brothers", several theologians set themselves to explain quite frankly what it meant to them "to be Catholic". At this point I shall simply take the illuminating analysis of one of them, Henri Denis, who suggests three main characteristics.

According to Denis, in the eyes of the Catholics, three criteria make their Church the Church of Christ:

1. The unity of the same faith, based on Scripture as interpreted by Tradition.

2. The celebration of the same sacraments (the seven which were listed at the Council of Trent).

3. Communion in the same apostolic ministry, that of all the bishops united with the Pope.

This last point is the most characteristic. If it is true that all the Churches, in varying degrees, have as their foundation the faith, the sacraments and the ministry, the distinctive characteristic of the Catholic Church is that "in the matter of tensions, conflicts and decisions to be taken or cases to be settled, it is always the ministry which has the final word and which prevails in the last resort." In concrete terms, this means the parish priest, the bishop and the pope, who is himself under the authority of Scripture, as Vatican II reminds us.

THE CONTINUITY OF CATHOLICISM

During the first centuries of the Roman Empire, when Christianity appeared on the scene, it appeared incarnated in a characteristic moral system. I believe that this moral system (this ethos as we used to say in the old days in Oxford to describe a moral doctrine practised by individuals) remains the living principle of contemporary Catholicism, that it is at the very heart of the Roman Church and is the guiding principle of all its activities. Outward cir-cumstances, the concrete conditions of its existence may change or remain the same. I will say just this, even supposing that its doctrine and government have changed, the ethos of the Catholic Church is still, even today, what it was in the past and whoever has a quarrel with the Catholicism of today is in fact opposed to that original ethos and had they lived 1800 years earlier, they would have quarrelled with the Christianity of the apostles and evangelists.

John Henry Newman, *Letters to Mosley*

124

The second distinguishing mark of being Catholic is having a sense of the faith as a whole, a sense of Christ as a living and integrating totality. This sense of Christ living today in the Church and in the world leads to a desire to encounter all cultures. It is this sense of Christ living in the Church which, according to Henri Denis, "makes Catholics practically always mindful of the fact that their Church has existed, through the risen Christ, since before the canon of Scripture was fixed."

The visibility of an institution is the third distinguishing mark. Compared with the Orthodox or Reformed Churches, the Catholic Church lays stress on visibility more than on 'mystique' or mere faith.

Finally the author tentatively asks the question, devoid of any sort of triumphalism: could not the Catholic Church, in imitation of the Anglican Church, play in the years to come the part of a 'bridge' between the "risky adventure" of the Reformed position and the "slightly rigid fidelity" of the Orthodox?

Let us add that, as in the case of the other Churches, there is darkness mixed in with the light for, very often, by stating its case with such clarity, the Church has presented a caricature of itself. Catholics should honestly admit that there are two areas in which their Church has not always avoided temptation.

1. The area of authority, where lack of moderation has sometimes ended in turning 'service' into 'power' and 'catholicity' into 'Romanism'. Immediately after the Council, the formidable Fr Bouyer took issue with the label 'Catholicism', a word which he believes first appeared in the seventeenth century. "If we mean by this, the artificial system forged by the Counter-Reformation and hardened by its confrontation with modernism, we shall be well rid of it. There is even a good chance that it is already gone, although we haven't yet noticed the fact."[35]

2. The area of relationships with the world where there has also been a lack of moderation. On the political level, compromise with the powerful. On the level of simple

faith, certain deviations of popular piety. On the level of a more 'intellectual' faith, the confusion between the authentic teaching of the faith and the theology belonging to a particular civilization and culture. (A striking example is the tendency, which we have not entirely lost, to raise the teachings of the mediaeval scholastics to the level of eternally valid truths.) These defects with regard to the Church's relationship with the world can lead to extremism on both progressive and traditionalist fronts. These remarks need not give Catholics a complex, but are meant to help them to avoid any return to the triumphalism of former times!

The Catholic Church today

Statistically, the Catholic Church is the largest of the Churches, with some 928.5 million faithful. These are to be found, though in unequal numbers, in all continents, with a predominance in the Western world, as may be seen from the following table which gives the percentage of Catholics in the total population of each continent.[36]

Africa:	88,899,000	(13.18%)
America :	461,264,000	(63.61%)
Asia:	86,012,000	(2.56%)
Europe:	285,294,000	(39.56%)
Oceania:	7,031,000	(26.51%)

As far as its structures and organization are concerned, the Catholic Church suffered certain repercussions from the various schisms of history. The schism with the East in 1054 isolated the Bishop of Rome, patriarch of the West, from the four other patriarchs. The result was that the Pope at present finds himself at the head of a Western patriarchate which Catholic missionaries have in effect extended to the four corners of the earth. In consequence, the 'patriarchal' function, which is intended to be exercised within a homogeneous culture and a limited geographical area, has come to be attached to the 'papal' function. This 'papal' function was quite separate in ancient times, and consisted merely in discreetly maintaining the communion between the other patriarchs of the universal Church in its diversity.

Later, new patriarchates appeared within this structure, which was both universal and Western. First, let us mention the Latin patriarchates, known as 'minor' (Jerusalem, Venice, Lisbon, Toledo, the West Indies and the East Indies). Those which have come down to the present day are mere historical survivals. More important are the Eastern Catholic patriarchates, the foremost of which is the Maronite Church of Lebanon which, since its creation in the twelfth century, has always remained directly and entirely attached to Rome. Elsewhere, there have been, since the seventeenth century, some parts of the Eastern Churches which have separated themselves from the Orthodox or from the ancient Eastern Churches and rejoined Rome, thus creating Eastern Catholic Churches, most of which have become parallel patriarchates.

Here is a list of these Churches, already mentioned, with a very approximate number of their adherents.

The Maronite Church:
   1,669,000 faithful (a third of whom are in the West).
The ancient Eastern Churches:
   in Mesopotamia: 280,000 Chaldeans;
   in Africa: 200,000 Copts and 110,000 Ethiopians.
In the Near East and South India:
   Syro-Malabar (2,800,000), Malankara (300,000), 100,000 Syrians.
In Armenia and in the Armenian diaspora:
   105,000 Armenians.

Coming from Orthodoxy (and including the Churches forcibly joined to Orthodoxy by the Communist regime, and which are in the process of regaining their independence):
In Europe:

4,340,000 Ukrainians, 462,000 Lithuanians,
3,000 Russians, 1,562,000 Romanians,
387,000 Czechs, 273,000 Hungarians,
7,000 Italo-Albanians, 2,700 Hellenic Greeks,
and 49,000 Yugoslavs;
In the Arabian Near East:
978,000 Melkites.

It is hard to generate ecumenical feeling amid this multiplicity of small Churches throughout the world, with their parallel hierarchies of Eastern Catholics and Eastern Orthodox. There is always the risk of animosity and rivalry so much at variance with the Gospel witness. One senses that new, ecumenical solutions must be found to these extremely complex problems.

Let us take a closer look, examining each point of view in turn. Today in the minds of the Orthodox – or the ancient Eastern Churches – the Uniate Churches are a constant reminder of what they consider as misplaced Roman proselytism, often accompanied by coercion and violence.

For the Catholic Church, on the other hand, the unions achieved in the Slav countries represent a certain success, albeit delayed and partial, of the scheme for unity agreed at the Council of Florence, a unity which did not last, but was always hoped for. How could such unity be renounced if the Churches concerned wanted it and were firmly attached to the idea? With a view to the future, the Second Vatican Council's *Decree on Eastern Catholic Churches* concludes that "all these directives of law are laid down in view of the present situation, until such time as the Catholic Church and the separated Eastern Churches come together into complete unity" (no. 30).

The Uniate Eastern Churches for their part – even if they feel that their uncomfortable situation cannot be a final solution – appreciate the link with Rome created by the centuries of common history, which has given them good quality priests, as well as help in resisting political and national pressures.

However, the situation is different for each of the Churches concerned. Let us take three examples.

The Greek Melkite Catholics of the Near East are in a most favourable situation as far as ecumenical progress is concerned. At the time of the Council, their Patriarch, Maximos IV, declared that they had a double mission: to show Catholics that Catholicism is not synonymous with Latinism; and to show the Eastern Christians that one can be united to the See of Peter without renouncing Orthodoxy or any of the spiritual treasures of the Orient. When this mission is complete, they will be able to disappear.[37] In the same patriarchate, the Catholic Archbishop of Baalbek, goes even further. He declares that he has a deep love for the Catholic Church, his Church, but that he also loves Orthodoxy and since it is impossible at present to be in full communion with Rome and the Orthodox Church at the same time, he maintains this double allegiance in his heart.[38]

However, the situation of the Uniate Church of Greece is very different. Their Church is small with 1,000 to 2,000 faithful and was only recently founded, and their relations with the Orthodox Church of Greece are difficult.[39]

Quite different again is the situation of the Churches of Eastern Europe, forcibly attached to the Orthodox Church immediately after the last war by the Communists. The problem has already been solved in the former Czechoslovakia during the Prague Spring of 1967.[40] At the time of writing, the question has not yet been settled in what was the former Soviet Union and in Romania, where difficult negotiations are now in progress. However, on both sides, courageous voices are being raised in favour of freedom and reconciliation and we must hope that they will be heeded. So Nicolas Lossky, of the exarchate of the patriarchate of Moscow in France, declares, "I believe that the Russian Church should acknowledge its sin. The violence that it suffered itself (at the turn of the sixteenth and seventeenth centuries) did not justify its complicity with the other sort of violence which came from the Stalinist regime."[41]

For his part, Cardinal Lubachivsky, chief archbishop of Lviv of the Ukrainians in exile, made a moving appeal in 1987, "Following the Spirit of Christ, we hold out the hand of forgiveness, reconciliation and love to the Russian people and the patriarchate of Moscow. As in our reconciliation with the people of Poland, we repeat Christ's words: 'Forgive us as we forgive' (Matthew 6:12). We are all brothers and sisters in Christ."[42]

As if echoing this appeal, the meeting in Moscow, in January 1990, between representatives of the Patriarchate of Moscow and the Holy See, worked towards "a normalization which should be the start of a new page in the history of Catholic-Orthodox relations. So we have asked that the conflicts and mutual injustices of the past be passed over in a spirit of sincere forgiveness and reconciliation, to give place to collaboration and the common witness to Jesus Christ which it is the Church's mission to proclaim."[43]

For it is indeed the evangelization of the world which should be the primary preoccupation. As the document *Baptism, Eucharist and Ministry* solemnly reminds us, "The Churches should seek a common answer to the following question: how, according to God's will and led by the Holy Spirit, should the life of the Church be conceived and ordered, so that the Gospel may be propagated and the community built up in love?"[44]

Without humiliating anyone, or causing anyone to deny their beliefs, it is possible to receive within oneself the attention to the Word of God, so cherished at the heart of the ecclesiastical families of the Reformation, and the spiritual treasures of the Orthodox Churches, along with all the charisms of the Catholic Church, setting oneself, day after day, to have confidence in the Mystery of the Faith.

Brother Roger of Taizé, *His love is a fire*

1. There have been more recent schisms both within Catholicism and in the Orthodox Church, beyond the scope of the present volume. Thus, within Orthodoxy, there were the Old Believers, a traditionalist reaction in the seventeenth century (2 or 3 million adherents); and, in the Catholic Church, the Old Catholics (a Church founded in 1889 from the union of the Jansenist Church of Utrecht and a group of Catholics led by the theologian Döllinger). They were opposed to the dogma of the infallibility of the Pope, proclaimed by Vatican I and have 500,000 to 700,000 adherents worldwide, with the recent addition of some of the faithful drawn into the schism of Archbishop Lefebvre, who was excommunicated in 1988.

2. Olivier Clément, *Dialogues avec le Patriarche Athénagoras*, Fayard, 1969, pp. 315-316.

3. Cf A monk of the Eastern Church, *The Jesus Prayer*, Chevetogne, 1963.

4. On the subject of the sometimes uninformed use of icons in the West, see the wise comments of the Episcopal Commission for Christian Unity: "The first seven councils and the use of icons" (*DC*, 19 July 1989, p. 773).

5. Yves Congar, "Nine hundred years on: notes on the Eastern schism", in *L'Église et les Églises*, Chevetogne 1954, vol. 1, p. 5.

6. A more detailed historical account and documentation may be found in the review *Istina*, particularly in the issue for January-March 1990: "The Union of Brest and the future of the Church of Ukraine". See also Yves Hamant, "The Ukraine and the Greek Catholic Church", in *Études*, September 1988.

7. Cf *The Orthodox Church in France: year book for 1990*, SOP, Courbevoie. For the self-governing Orthodox communities as for all the Christian Churches to be mentioned later, the statistics are difficult to establish. A reliable source of information is the monumental *World Christian encyclopaedia: a comparative survey of Churches and religions in the modern world, AD 1900-2000*, Oxford University Press, Nairobi 1982. We shall refer to this unless there is a more recent or more accurate source available. According to the sources consulted, the numbers are highly variable and can range from single to double figures. Those of the Eastern countries are very uncertain at the moment.

8. Yves Congar, *Diversités et communion*, Cerf 1982, p. 133.

9. This is also the attitude of the Catholic Church. The "Directory for the application of the Second Vatican Council's teaching on ecumenism" included a reminder of the friendly position of the Council. Eucharistic hospitality is considered possible; a Catholic who attends an Orthodox Mass fulfils the Sunday obligation; in case of need, a Catholic may confess to an Orthodox priest, etc. (*DC*, 18 June 1967, col. 1085-1086). However, there is no corresponding welcome from the Orthodox side, notably in eucharistic hospitality, which usually obliges Catholics to abstain from communion.

10. Sermon in Notre Dame in Paris, 5 June 1983, in *SOP*, pp. 12-13.

11. Cardinal Joseph Ratzinger, *The principles of Catholic theology: outline and materials*, Téqui 1985, p. 22.
12. *DC* , 19 January 1975, p. 63.
13. "Documents on the dialogue on charity" in *Tomos Agapis*, Rome-Istanbul 1971. *The Livre de la charité*, Cerf 1984 repeats 60 of the 284 documents of *Tomos Agapis* and adds 34 for the period 1970-1978.
14. See Jean Corbon, *L'Église des Arabes*, Cerf 1977, chapter II, "Le visage et le mystère"; Emmanuel-Pataq Siman, *L'expérience de l'Esprit par l'Église, d'après la tradition syrienne d'Antioche*, Beauchesne 1971; Irne-Henri Dalmais, *Liturgies d'Orient: rites et symboles*, Cerf 1980.
15. *Episkepsis*, 14 March 1972, pp. 4-6, and 5 March 1990, pp. 3-4. See also Bernard Dupuy, "Où en est le dialogue entre l'Orthodoxie et les Églises dites monophysites?", in *Istina*, April-June 1990, with the text of various declarations.
16. *DC*, 7 October 1951, col. 1226 and col. 1239.
17. *DC*, 2 September 1984, pp. 825-826.
18. Lothar Wolleh, *The Second Vatican Council*, in collaboration with Père Emile Schnitz, Vatican Radio. Introduction by Cardinal Eugène Tisserant 1966 (Edito-service S.A., Geneva), p. 50. Pope John Paul II spoke in the same vein during his visit to Germany in 1980, "We do not wish to judge one another (Romans 14:13). On the contrary, we wish to acknowledge our faults together" (*DC*, 21 December 1980, p. 1146).
19. In Ludwig von Pastor, *History of the Popes from the close of the Middle Ages* , Plon 1913, volume IX, pp. 104-105.
20. *Semaine Religieuse du diocèse de Marseilles*, 6 November 1983.
21. *BIP*, 21 February 1990. André Thobois says in this article that the number of baptized should be multiplied by three to obtain the number of parishioners. That would give some 100 million people in the 'Baptist family' (Jean Baubrot, *Le retour des Huguenots*, p. 205).
22. Cf at the theological level, the famous thesis of Hans Küng, *Justification: the doctrine of Karl Barth: a Catholic reflection* (Burns and Oates), which concludes that there is no fundamental difference between the doctrine of justification as set forth by the Council of Trent and that of the Protestant theologian Karl Barth.
    At the level of dialogue, the document published in 1983 by the Catholic-Lutheran dialogue group, came to the positive conclusion that the two positions were in basic agreement (*DC*, 20 January 1985). A commission of the German Episcopal Conference and the Evangelical Lutheran Church in Germany, set up after John Paul II's first visit to Germany in 1980, has recently published its final report, which concludes that the doctrinal condemnations of the sixteenth century no longer apply to the fellow-Christians of today. *Les anathèmes du XVIe siècle sont-ils encore actuels?* Cerf, 1989.
23. "Consensus oecuménique et différence fondamentale: réflections et propositions du Comité mixte catholique-protestante en France", *DC*, 4 January 1987, p. 44.
24. *BSS*, 27 March 1985. Also in *BSS*, 11 January 1989, the report of the joint Catholic-Protestant committee on the message of the four synods

of the reformed Church which "expressed wishes or were the occasion of pronouncements which, doubtless unintentionally, were seen as instruments of confusion, aggressiveness and anti-Catholic feeling, whatever anyone may say".

25. *DC*, 5 March 1978.
26. The Catholic-Lutheran International Commission, *Face à l'unité: tous les textes officiels (1972 -1985)*, Cerf, 1986, p. 368ff.
27. Yves Congar, "Bulletin d'ecclésiologie oecuménique", in *Revue des sciences philosophiques et théologiques*, January 1987, p. 127.
28. *Jalons pour l'unité: The Final Report of the Anglican-Roman Catholic International Commission*, Cerf, 1982. The Anglican Church, after discussions at the Lambeth Conference in 1988, gave a positive reply. The Catholic Church replied in 1991, underlining the significant contribution of the text, but demanding supplementary clarifications concerning the Catholic doctrine on the Eucharist and ordained ministry (Text in *DC*, 2 February 1992). Some extreme demands concerning the formulation have roused astonishment in ecumenical circles (see the article by J. de Baciocchi, "La foi et sa formulation" in *La Croix*, 4 March 1992).
29. *DC*, 15 March 1987.
30. *DC*, 6 April 1986, p. 355.
31. *Jalons pour l'unité*, op. cit., p. 95.
32. *DC*, 5 November, 1989, p. 938.
33. *Unité des Chrétiens*, special issue on the Catholic Church, April 1986, pp. 2-4.
34. A majority of two-thirds was required in each of the three (bishops, clergy and laity) Synod Houses. The result was: House of Bishops: 75%; House of Clergy (priests and deacons, the latter including men and women): 70%; House of Laity: only 67%.
35. Louis Bouyer, *La décomposition du catholicisme*, Aubier 1968, p. 152.
36 *Omnis Terra*, November 1992, p. 465.
37. Emilios Inglessis, *Maximos IV conteste l'Occident*, Cerf, 1969, p. 39. See also Joseph Hajjar, *Les chrétiens uniates du Proche-Orient*, Seuil, 1962.
38. Elias Zoghby, *Tous schismatiques?*, Beirut, 1981, p. 150.
39. Cf the final remarks in the article by Emmanuel Lanne, "United Churches or sister Churches?" in *Irénikon*, 1970/3, pp. 338ff, "The uniate Churches have a right to our respect... Their members have a role to play in the rebuilding of unity... But the existence of an apostolic exarchate of the Greek rite with a bishop appointed by Rome is the negation of the recognition of the sister Church of Greece... We have to get beyond the idea of united Churches to that of sister Churches, by taking seriously articles 14 and 17 of the decree on ecumenism."
40. Cf the article by Michel Lacko in *Istina*, 1973, p. 48ff.
41. Interview in *Actualité religieuse dans le monde*, 15 January 1988, p. 29.
42. *DC*, 21 February 1988, p. 227. For a review of the problem as a whole, see the special issue of *Istina*, 1990/1, "The Union of Brest (1596) and the future of the Church of the Ukraine".
43. *DC*, 1 April 1990, p. 347.
44. *BEM*, op. cit., p. 49.

Chapter 5

A glance towards
the future

YOU will have noticed that the main theme of this book is that the ecumenical movement, which is now irreversible, has reached the point where it will make no further progress without a certain *metanoia* on the part of all the Churches. This is slowly taking place before our eyes. This last chapter returns to this subject, stressing two important points: the area in which this *metanoia* should occur, and the unity which we can now see taking shape.

1. There is in each Church an important area which should be explored by all the other Churches

The questions the Churches ask each other are many, and are not all of equal importance. They do not always query the same point and it sometimes happens that they are contradictory. It also happens that they converge. When they are contradictory, one is tempted to judge in favour of neither Church, without hearing the case any further. Let us take for example the cult of the saints and the veneration of relics. Protestants vigorously denounce this practice, while the Orthodox take it even further than the Catholics. So here we have two viewpoints which make it impossible for the dialogue amongst the Churches in general to reach any conclusion.

It is a different matter if the Churches with which one is in dialogue all query the same point of a particular issue. In this case, one is led to think that this unanimity represents a question that is at once unavoidable and complex. When a

Church constantly incurs the criticism of all the other Churches on a specific point to which it has always held, sometimes at great cost, one can conclude two things.

On the one hand, it is an indication that this point is in fact the most important point of faith for this particular Church and therefore constitutes its irremovable part of the truth, to which it feels bound in conscience and on which it is unable ever to yield. It means, then, that this point, which is so foreign to the other Churches, could well be the 'contribution' of that Church to all the others. However, at the same time, if all the Churches are united in their criticism of this point, it is obvious that there is need for conversion in this area, where the Church concerned cannot refuse a bold re-examination of its language and behaviour. In other words, the irremovable part of the truth of each Church is also the area of its temptation, and so of its *metanoia*. Let us now consider particular cases.

First, the Catholic Church. It is undeniable that the Catholic Church is criticized by all the Churches (Protestants, Orthodox, ancient Eastern Churches, Anglicans and Old Catholics) on the authority of the Bishop of Rome (the way in which it is defined and has been exercised throughout history, with all the implications of its 'primacy', etc.). If we accept the reasoning proposed above, it would mean that the tenacious insistence of Rome, in affirming and consolidating this authority, corresponds to the irremovable part of truth of the Catholic Church. This, therefore, is its 'contribution' to all the other Churches. However, at the same time, the fact that all the other Churches, despite their differences, unite in criticizing Rome on this point, means that the Catholic Church needs to revise and purify its definition of this authority and the way it is exercised.

One of the fruits of the ecumenical movement is the bringing to our attention the many positive signs that people are recognizing this line of reasoning. We have already noted the declaration of the Patriarch Dimitrios, in 1975, when Pope Paul VI kissed the feet of his envoy, Metropolitan Meliton; and the Archbishop of Canterbury's declaration at Lambeth in 1988 and in Rome in 1989, as signs of an acceptance of a ministry by the Bishop of Rome as a means of drawing all the Churches into communion with the Orthodox and with the Anglicans. We could also mention other instances.

Similar opinions have been voiced by the Reformed Churches. Karl Barth confided one day to Monsignor Elchinger that if the primacy of the Pope corresponded to the way it had been exercised by John XXIII and Paul VI – not a boss who wants to rule in every area, but one who 'presides in charity', a servant of the Word of God and of unity – we could no doubt come to some sort of agreement.[1]

Similarly, the Lutherans in the Lutheran-Catholic work group in the United States would accept a primacy in which the relationship of the pope with the Lutheran Churches was more pastoral than juridical. Here, the pontifical primacy would be "structured and interpreted in such a way that it would clearly serve the Gospel and the unity of the Church of Christ, and its authority exercised in such a way that Christian liberty was not endangered."[2]

In the same vein, Jean-Jacques von Allmen writes that Rome does not need to renounce its claim to primacy, but to exercise it in a spirit of humility, without clinging to the "dust of empire", nor trying to be the Secretary General of the universal Church, but taking the local Churches and episcopal conferences seriously. The Catholic Church, he adds, should open up for general discussion the doctrinal decisions which have been made in *statu divisionis*.[3]

This last request is now being made by Catholic theologians also. In a powerful and timely book, Fr Tillard expresses his hope that the pronouncements of Vatican I might be re-assessed in the light of ecumenism. This process was already begun at Vatican II and certain elements in Vatican I itself, hitherto little noticed, could justify such a venture.[4] Also, it is interesting to note that the declaration *Mysterium Ecclesiae*, the aim of which is to guard against opinions opposed to the primacy, contains a lengthy section on the need to take into account "the historical conditions" under which dogmatic pronouncements are made, which means that "the ideas of one particular period may leave their mark on any doctrinal pronouncements."[5]

Concerning a reform in which the authority of the Bishop of Rome is expressed and exercised, who could deny there is a movement, both in general style and in practical application, towards decentralization? Theologians have analysed the most important points. The Dombes text on the ministry to the universal Church starts by studying the historical evolution of Roman authority during the first millennium and then during the second, after the great schisms. At the end of their reflections, their "Proposals for a conversion (*metanoia*) of the Catholic Church" are clear, balanced and courageous. We quote a few key passages here:

148. In accordance with the whole tradition, we believe that it is in virtue of his role as Bishop of Rome that the Pope exercises a special ministry towards the universal Church and that this ministry is necessary to the structure of the Church.

149. In a spirit of *metanoia* we wish that the dogmatic expression of this ministry, which has been in force since Vatican I and which deeply wounds the Christian feelings of our separated brethren of the East and West, might now be reformulated and brought up-to-date so that it could form part of an ecclesiology of communion. The ancient tradition of the Church witnesses to such an effort at the constant improvement of the language of faith, with 'corrections' to be made where necessary, in order to present it in a more balanced perspective.

150. In the same spirit, we should also wish to see the renewal of the outward expression of the papal ministry of communion in the Church.

151. We do not, however, wish to see an impoverishment or weakening of the personal ministry of com-

munion of the universal Church. With regard to those who have exercised this ministry in the past, who do so today and will do so in the future, we desire them to do so in the full light of the Gospel. This ministry should remain as a source of initiative, new ideas and general support for all the Churches as they stand out against the hostility of the world and the pressures exerted by certain governments.[6]

Let us now look at the Churches which grew out of the Reformation: the Lutherans, the Reformed and the Evangelical. These Churches are questioned by all other Christians on their conception of freedom in relation to the apostolic ministry. Indeed, even among the Churches of the Reformation, the Lutherans would query the Reformed and Evangelicals on this point. Following a reasoning similar to that we used before, we could conclude that the tenacious insistence of the Churches of the Reformation on the freedom of the Gospel and the Spirit, throughout the course of history, is their irremovable part of the truth and their 'contribution' to all the Churches.

However, at the same time, all the other Churches are united in questioning the freedom adopted by the Churches of the Reformation with regard to the 'apostolic ministry'; this can only show that there is need for a review here. A too radical approach to evangelical freedom has led to the rejection, not only of the related ecclesiastical structures, but also of those basic structures linked to the apostolic ministry by the laying on of hands, which the other Churches generally express by the continuity of an episcopate.

As in the Catholic Church, one can find signs that this last viewpoint is being reviewed in the process of ecclesiastical self-examination facilitated by the ecumenical movement. Thus the dialogue between the Lutheran World Federation and the Catholic Church clearly shows that the Lutherans are taking the question of apostolic ministry seriously. While the Catholics were making recommendations to their own Church, the Protestant signatories of the same Dombes text, for their part, were making their own suggestions which were equally clear, balanced and courageous:

153. In the measure in which the Church of Rome is today renouncing the privileges of a powerful primacy and centralization and embarking instead on the way to a primacy of service and unity in the faith, this attitude of *metanoia* poses a crucial challenge to all the Churches, which none of them can evade.

158. Various dialogues between Lutherans, Anglicans and Catholics have helped us all to think deeply about a personal form of ministry in the whole of the universal Church. Should not the Churches of the Reformation look into this question of a personal ministry in such a way that they both witness to their own heritage and open themselves to this concept of ministry?

160. In order to go further along this same path, it would be helpful to take another look at the guidelines set down by the Dombes Group in 1976 for a deeper appreciation of an apostolic ministry. What resulted from those guidelines? Has not all our research, however useful, on the question of the diversification of the ministry, somewhat eclipsed the indispensable rediscovery of an episcopal ministry without which this diversification will inevitably lead to the splitting up of the community?[7]

I have dwelt at length on the mutual questioning of the Catholic and Reformation Churches because it is the most prominent. Let us now move on to the Orthodox Church. What we have already said should clearly show the irremovable part of the truth represented by its spiritual and liturgical message, and its need to examine its relationship to the world and to history, and the need for continuous reform. Reflecting on the presence of Baptist Churches in Russia, Olivier Clément once pondered on what an in-depth dialogue with the Orthodox Church could bring to both sides. On the one hand, there would be the freshness of the Gospel and the missionary fervour of the first Christian communities as described in the Acts of the Apostles. This was when the Church had not yet had to take up a position on the apostolic ministry and its structures, as they were still living in the apostolic age. On the other, there was the treasures of a thousand-year-old liturgy and a tradition of sanctity and ecclesiastical structure (with the need which traditionally-minded Churches have to give a clear witness to the Gospel).[8]

WHAT CHURCHMEN LACK

What churchmen most lack is the spirit of Christ, humility, the dispossession of self, a disinterested welcome to others, the capacity to see the best in others. We are afraid, we want to keep things that are out-of-date because we are used to them, we want to be in the right, we hide a spirit of pride and power beneath conventional expressions of humility. We stand aloof from real life. We have made of the Church an organization like any other. All our energies have gone into setting it up, now we spend them on keeping it going. And it functions, more or less, less rather than more, but it does function. Only it functions like a machine. Like a machine and not like a living thing.

Patriarch Athenagoras, in O. Clément,
Dialogues with Patriarch Athenagoras, pp. 154-155

In the same way, how many complicated questions Catholic and Orthodox have for one another, such as the benefit of having a primacy in the West (which still lacks a synodal system) and that of having a synodal system in the East (which still lacks a primacy at the universal level). Looking at the future from this angle might give rise to a particular anxiety. If the changes proposed in all these dialogues actually took place, would there not be a kind of uniform levelling of the Churches? We must answer firmly in the negative, for the aim of the ecumenical movement is not a monolithic unity but a unity in communion, in fruitful multiformity.

2. Towards full communion

Let us look towards the future and dream a little. The goal to which all the Churches aspire can be nothing less than a 'communion' in which each Church will keep its "irremovable part of the truth" and will accept the need for a *metanoia* which will transform the divisive differences into a diversity compatible with communion. Briefly, let us say that this would involve the acceptance by all of certain aspects of Church life. For example, a ministry of communion by the Bishop of Rome in the service of the universal Church would be the contribution of the Catholic Church. A decentralized synodal system as practised by the Orthodox and Anglicans would be accepted, as would an episcopal ministry, considered as essential by Catholics, Orthodox and Anglicans. There would also be a demand for freedom which is at the very heart of the Reformed and Anglican Churches. The complementarity of these demands would guard against this communion becoming a rampant form of 'absorption', which is still perhaps secretly desired both by ardent supporters of uniformity and by advocates of unlimited pluralism.

An ecclesiology of 'communion', we need hardly be reminded, is profoundly biblical. The word *koinonia* signifies the solemn entry of each baptized person and of each believing community into the area of reconciliation opened up by Christ on the cross and revealed by the Spirit in the light of Pentecost. Fr Tillard explains this process as "The first Johannine letter goes so far as to say, 'Our communion is a communion with the Father and his Son Jesus Christ'

(John 1:3). In this sense, Christians are *sun-koinonoi* (cf. Philippians 1:7; Revelation 1:9). This amounts almost to a definition of the Christian and an affirmation of salvation."[9] The biblical term 'communion' has the advantage of being able to include all the concrete situations of today, at whatever stage of progress they may be. It is an expression which is starting to come to the attention of all the Churches.

Since its assembly in Budapest in 1984, the Lutheran World Federation has given a central place to reflection on the concept of communion and took this as the inspiration for its new statutes, adopted at the assembly in Curitiba (Brazil) in February 1990. A recent study at the Centre for Ecumenical Studies in Strasbourg developed this theme, touching on its biblical sources, historical use and application to all the Churches in the ecumenical context of the present day.[10]

The Roman Synod of 1985 suggested that the Catholic Church be defined as a communion "with God, through Jesus Christ, in the Holy Spirit", of which the Eucharist is the source and highest point, in which "one and the same Spirit is at work through various spiritual gifts and many different charisms" (cf Corinthians 12:4ff), and in which the various Churches manifest "multiformity in unity" which is quite different from mere pluralism.[11] The synod also suggested that the path of ecumenism was in fact a passage from an incomplete communion, already in existence in varying degrees, according to the Churches in question, to the full communion of the future (no. 7). Already in Geneva, in 1969, Pope Paul VI, having reminded us that his name was 'Peter', was affirming that he conceived of his ministry as a "ministry of communion".[12]

Let us continue to dream, and, since we need images in order to think, let us look at what the Christian imagination has sketched out as "models of unity" for the progressive realization of communion. Some of the models recommended by the Churches of the Reformation (such as the formulae of "doctrinal agreement" or "plural unity", etc.) have proved useful for talks between themselves, but would seem inadequate to the other Churches. Several other models have been suggested, more acceptable to the other families of Churches.

At the Assembly of the World Council in Nairobi in 1975, it was an Orthodox, Fr Cyrille Argenti, who suggested the formula "conciliar community of local Churches, themselves authentically united". Naturally, the formula would need to be explained further. It seemed to the Protestants to be too 'Catholic', and it could not be accepted by the Catholics unless it was made clear that the local Churches would be led by bishops in communion with the Bishop of Rome. Yet, the formula contains seeds of hope for the future.[13]

It was Cardinal Willebrands, then president of the Roman Secretariat for Unity, who suggested the formula "*types of Churches*". The idea is that of a possible plurality of 'types' within the communion of Christian Churches. It is based on a statement of the Council reminding us that "various Churches established in diverse place by the Apostles and their successors have in the course of time coalesced into several groups, organically united, which, preserving the unity of faith and the unique divine constitution of the universal Church, enjoy their own discipline, their own liturgical usage, and their own theological and spiritual heritage."[14] The Council applies this definition to the ancient patriarchal Churches and their off-shoots, but since Cardinal Willebrands should have chosen to refer to it several times, always in the context of the dialogue with the Anglican Church, clearly shows his intention to make it a model of possible unity between that Church and the Catholic Church.[15] Also, this brings us back to the idea of an "Anglican Church, united but not absorbed", rejected by Rome at the time of the Malines Conversations, in 1925, but taken up again, word for word, by Paul VI, in 1977.[16]

A third model, of Protestant origin, has been suggested by the Lutheran Harding Meyer, that of "reconciled diversity". The formula may seem similar to that of "plural unity" if one puts the emphasis on diversity considered as static. However, its originator has protested against this reductionist interpretation, explaining that reconciled diversity implies a "redefinition of the various confessions by means of dialogue" and that it calls for specific acts of reconciliation.[17] All the Churches can agree to tread a path which includes dialogue and reciprocal conversion.

Things will doubtless turn out differently from the way we have imagined them, but these models suffice to show that the way forward lies open: stage by stage and by gradual degrees, there will be a fuller and fuller communion between all the Churches.

WE ARE GOING ROUND IN CIRCLES

The members of the Anglican-Roman Catholic Commission have shown that the moment has come to move on to a new and crucial phase of the dialogue initiated fifteen years ago, to pass on from a time of research to a time of decisions on the part of their respective Churches. Otherwise we shall be in danger of going round in circles, detracting from the dynamism of the ecumenical movement and making it sterile.

Cardinal Willebrands in Baltimore, 20 October 1982

After our dream, let us fly to even greater heights! Is not the most beautiful kind of communion the one which unites those who are in the etymological sense witnesses, the martyrs of all the Churches? A chapel in Canterbury Cathedral has been dedicated to these 'martyrs', our contemporaries of the twentieth century, a list to which names are still being added. They belong to the Catholic, Orthodox, Anglican and Protestant Churches. They are:
- Charles de Foucauld (1916);
- Metropolitan Vladimir of Kiev (1917);
- Patriarch Tikhon of all Russia (1925);

- Maximilian Kolbe (1941);
- Edith Stein (1942);
- Vivian Redlich and Lucian Tapiedi (1942);
- Maria Skobtsova (1945);
- Dietrich Bonhoeffer (1945);
- Jonathan Daniels (1965);
- Martin Luther King (1968);
- Archbishop Janani Luwum (1977);
- Archbishop Oscar Romero (1980);
- Bahram William Dehgani-Tafti (1980);
- Arastoo Sayyah-Sina (1979).

They laid down their lives in the service of the Gospel. May they inspire us to make the sacrifices necessary for the realization of communion.

NOTES

1. *DC*, 2 March 1969, p. 249.
2. *DC*, 21 April 1974, p. 379.
3. Jean-Jacques von Allmen, *La primauté de l'Église de Pierre et de Paul*, Cerf, 1977, p. 107.
4. J.M.R. Tillard, *L'évêque de Rome*, Cerf, 1982, pp. 28-29.
5. The declaration *Mysterium Ecclesiae* on the doctrine concerning the Church with a view to protecting it from the errors of the present day. *DC*, 15 July 1973, p. 667.
6. *Pour la communion des Eglises*, op. cit., pp. 215-216.
7. Ibid., p. 217-220.
8. Olivier Clément, *L'esprit de Soljenitsyne*, Stock 1974.
9. J.M.R. Tillard, *Église d'Églises: l'ecclésiologie de communion*, Cerf, 1987, pp. 35 and 36.
10. *Communion/Koinonia*, Une prise de position du Centre d'Études Oecuméniques de Strasbourg, 1990.
11. *DC*, 5 January 1986, p. 41.
12. *DC*, 6 July 1969, p. 625.
13. *DC*, 15 February 1976, p. 175.
14. *Constitution on the Church*, no. 23.
15. *DC*, 3 December 1972, p. 1066.
16. *DC*, 15 May 1977, p. 457.
17. Cf appendix to Yves Congar's, *Diversités et communion*, Cerf, 1982, p. 231.

Conclusion

THE reconstruction of the history of the separation of the Churches, following the unbiassed research undertaken by ecumenical discussion groups, teaches us several lessons. This history allows us to see the importance of political, social and cultural contexts; and we are now discovering the significant part played by misunderstandings after we have lived with them for centuries. Gradually, we are beginning to see that responsibility was often divided between the Churches in conflict and that their confrontations hardly bore witness to the Gospel. Which does not mean, however, that there were no justifiable reasons for such attitudes, on both sides. For history also confirms the theological problems which arose in complex situations were neither artificial nor frivolous. For, profound matters of faith were at stake and the Churches clung tenaciously to their positions, sometimes to the point of rigidity and distortion. It is thus that a caricature at once masks and reveals the true face.

If we desire full communion between all the Churches, we simply must take all this into account, without juggling with the facts, for God has no need of our lies (Job 13:7). Nor should we pharisaically judge our forebears (Luke 18:9ff), but should rather look resolutely to the future. The grace of our age is that the process of restoration of communion between the Churches is already under way, even if not everyone is yet aware of this.

In conclusion, let us therefore stress the three stages which are necessary for the development of ecumenical awareness in a Christian – and also in a Church.

The first stage is to get to know the other Churches better, all of them, and not just the one which is near at hand. Experience shows that often we have little knowledge of the other Churches and that certain denominational writings continue to spread errors. These allow Christian people to harbour incredible caricatures of other Churches in their collective memory.

However, this better mutual acquaintance is but the first step, because it is possible to know the other persons, even to know them well, while still despising them a little and avoiding meeting them too often. So the second stage is to accept a certain mystery in the other Churches, in their faithfulness to Jesus Christ. Of course this does not mean putting everything on the same level. A certain feature of another Church may seem not only strange and confusing, but totally unacceptable. Even so, ecumenism teaches respect for that other Church's mysterious faithfulness, which is linked to its irremovable part of the truth. At this stage, dialogue, communal action and an intelligent common witness, are not only possible, but necessary. The service of our brothers and sisters is urgently needed and Christians, even though separated, are called to do together everything that their consciences allow. This is clearly a monumental task.

However, to stop at this point would be laziness, because there is one last step to be taken. One can in fact readily admire the other Churches and work with them, while remaining, on both sides, comfortably entrenched in the status quo, perfectly satisfied with one's own Church as it is. So the third stage of ecumenism will be to emerge from this inertia and to accept the challenge of the other Church to a deeper fidelity to the Gospel. All through these pages, we have seen that initiatives of this kind are beginning to take place in nearly all the Churches.

We are only at the beginning, and the road is strewn with obstacles. In all the Churches, there are 'terrorist' minorities, some traditionalist, some liberal, which are trying to lay snares in the way, which sometimes means that the leaders of these Churches have their hands tied. Also, it often happens that there is a lack of confidence. Each Church has a vague fear that its own move towards *metanoia* may lead to a secret triumphalism on the part of the others. It should also be said that sometimes things go so quickly that the best of people begin to take fright, wondering anxiously where all this is going to lead us. But how could it be otherwise? In some ways, our age is in the process of living, in reverse, all that happened at the time of separation, with the worried feeling one has when landmarks are changed and one no longer knows exactly where one is.

In order to achieve ecumenical progress, there is always one determining factor: the experience of being evangelized by a brother or sister from the other Church.

> Witness of a pastor and priest, *Unité des chrétiens*,
> January 1982, p. 20

We have need of clear confidence. We also need courage and discernment. We must listen to the Spirit who urges us forward, and also to young people who ask us to make haste. We need not implement all the ideas of the young, but we should always remember that, with their fresh vision, they act in a way as the radar of tomorrow's world. When we have at last achieved full communion, the younger generation will say to us, "How easy it was! How can it possibly have taken you so long to sort things out?" If we keep our ears open, we shall be able to hear them saying it already.

GROWING CLOSER TOGETHER

Rome and Canterbury: a relationship of hope

Maria J. Van Dyck

A clear, simple, yet scholarly account of the events that led the English Church to break away from Rome and of the various ecumenical efforts and movements since to heal the rift. After examining the forces and factors that caused the English Church's break with Rome, the book studies the relationship between Anglicans and Catholics from the 16th to the 20th century, then focuses on the ARCIC statement 'Authority in the Church' (1976-1982) and its significance for Anglican-Catholic dialogue in the present century.

As Henry Chadwick says in his foreword to the book, historical method alone cannot bring about reconciliation where fundamental dogma is at stake. Yet without an awareness of the past debates there can be no real progress in dialogue. This awareness is what Maria Van Dyck offers the reader, which ends with the image of Pope John Paul II and Archbishop Robert Runcie praying together – a symbol of the sharing of love and authority in the hoped for one Church of Christ.

MARIA J. VAN DYCK is a member of the Canonical Order of the Holy Sepulchre in Turnhout Priory (Belgium). She is a Doctor of Sciences in Zoology and a lector emeritus of the Catholic University of Louvain where she graduated in Theology and obtained a doctorate in 1989 for her dissertation 'Church and Authority'. Since 1989 she has been giving lectures in ecumenical subjects throughout Belgium.

267 pages   ISBN 085439 402 8   £9.95

ONE IN 2000?

Paul McPartlan

Here, for the first time, the agreed statements of
the Catholic-Orthodox international commission for
dialogue are made widely available, with an introduction by its Catholic co-secretary and a foreword
by one of its leading Orthodox members.

Accompanying papers describe the historical,
theological and spiritual context within which the
Catholic and Orthodox Churches are striving to be
One in 2000.

PAUL MCPARTLAN is a priest of the Diocese of West-
minster. After a theological licence in Rome, he gained
his doctorate at Oxford comparing Catholic and Orthodox understanding of the Eucharist.

182 pages   ISBN 085439 439 7   £7.25

THINGS OLD AND NEW

*An ecumenical reflection
on the theology of John Henry Newman*

Emmanuel Sullivan

Things old and new shows in a clear and convincing way how the three characteristic elements in Newman's thinking about the tradition of the Church, the development of doctrine and the need to consult the faithful can be keys to understanding contemporary puzzles on the ecumenical agenda. What it says about receiving the fruits of ecumenical dialogue in the life of our Churches and about the approach to the question of the ordination of women is helpful and healing. Its great contribution lies in the insights it gives to the ecumenical pilgrimage in the last decade of this century. If these ecumenical lessons drawn from Newman's writings can be learnt we shall continue together, Anglicans and Roman Catholics, within the wider ecumenical movement towards the visible unity of the one, holy, catholic and apostolic Church.

EMMANUEL SULLIVAN *is a Franciscan Friar of the Atonement. Since 1967 he has been active in ecumenical ministry. and helped establish an ecumenical community and centre at Hengrave Hall in Suffolk. He was a visiting scholar at St Edmund's House, Cambridge. In 1984 he became director of the Graymoor Ecumenical Institute. Recently he has been appointed ecumenical officer to the RC Diocese of Arundel and Brighton.*

160 pages   ISBN 085439 438 9   £7.95

CHURCH AND HUMAN RIGHTS

Jean-François Six

Human rights have become the most important topic of debate and controversy in recent times. In this book, which is written in the form of a closely argued dialogue, the author traces the evolution of the concept of human rights both in Church and society.

There has been a profound shift of emphasis in political, social and religious thinking. The Church is engaged in the difficult task of appraising its position on religious freedom, which has a great bearing on the role of Christianity in today's society. Thus the advancement of human rights is the true test of dialogue between the Church and the modern world.

The book ends with a call for greater democracy at the very heart of the Church itself so that it would be more effective in promoting human rights in the world.

JEAN-FRANÇOIS SIX, *a priest of the French Mission, is a historian and theologian. He is the founder of the organisation Human Rights and Solidarity which works for the recognition of human rights in everyday life in society.*

120 pages   ISBN 085439 368 4   £5.50

CHARISMS
AND NEW EVANGELIZATION

Paul Joseph Cordes

In his First Letter to the Thessalonians, St Paul admonished them not to suppress the Spirit or despise inspired messages, but to put all things to the test and keep what is good. In this Decade of Evangelization, Archbishop Paul Joseph Cordes has the same message for the universal Church.

We are witness to the action of the Holy Spirit in the Charismatic Renewal Movement, the Neocatechumenals, the Cursillo Movement, Communion and Liberation, the Focolare Movement, and many others. But the Church today, as in the time of St Paul, has difficulty in allowing such movements of the Spirit to operate freely. Yet, as *Charisms and new evangelization* reminds us, the Lord gives charisms to men and women so that they may effectively engage in the process of new evangelization, which is the true test of the Church's involvement in the world.

The book also emphasises the responsibility of the Church's hierarchy in recognizing and fostering these charisms in the community of believers. We are warned not to muffle the voice of the Spirit.

PAUL JOSEPH CORDES, *born in Germany in 1934, was ordained priest in 1961 and was made auxiliary bishop of Paderborn in 1975. In 1980 Pope John Paul II appointed him Vice President of the Pontifical Council for the Laity. The pope has personally given Archbishop Cordes the responsibility of following the apostolate of the International Catholic Charismatic Renewal and the Neocatechumenal Community.*

172 pages   ISBN 085439 403 6   £5.95